S0-GGP-434

TOWN GOVERNMENT IN THE
SIXTEENTH CENTURY

TOWN GOVERNMENT IN THE SIXTEENTH CENTURY

*Based chiefly on the records of the following
provincial towns*

CAMBRIDGE, CHESTER, COVENTRY, IPSWICH, LEICESTER,
LINCOLN, MANCHESTER, NORTHAMPTON, NORWICH,
NOTTINGHAM, OXFORD, SHREWSBURY

by

J. H. THOMAS

B.LITT.(OXON)

ILLUSTRATED

LONDON
GEORGE ALLEN & UNWIN LTD
MUSEUM STREET

FIRST PUBLISHED IN 1933

PREFACE

THIS short survey of early municipal government, based on town records, is put forward for several reasons. It deals with an interesting period in municipal government, and gives a picture of the old English town that is different from that usually given. It also reveals the close connection between social experiment and national legislation. Sixteenth-century town authorities were small groups trying to solve local problems, and their solutions could be, and were, applied on a national scale. To-day the national authorities welcome local experiments for social ills in the hope that some national solution will evolve.

Town records are minutes of the meetings of the ruling authority. Practical questions of local government are seldom decided at one meeting, but may be discussed for months, so a picture of town life drawn from old records is a piecing together of bits from many discussions. Because of this and because published town records are in chronological order, in this book a simple method of reference for all important statements has been secured by mentioning the town and year in the text, and as a complete list of the records used is given at the end of the book, the student should not have difficulty in tracing a reference. Where a statement cannot be easily traced in this way or where it is not from town records the reference is given.

I take this opportunity of thanking the many people who have assisted me since I joined the adult education movement. I owe much to the Yorkshire W.E.A., and especially to members of the Keighley branch, where the late J. R. Taylor, M.A., was my guide for many years. At Manchester the late Professor Unwin introduced me to the study of local records, and at Oxford E. Lipson, M.A., did much to make my work easy.

My thanks are specially due to Dr. R. H. Tawney and to R. H. Hodgkin, M.A., of Queen's College, Oxford, for assistance on many occasions; to the Oxford University Delagacy for Advanced Studies; the Delagacy for Extra-Mural Studies; and the Queen's College, for having made possible the publication of this work.

J. H. T.

CONTENTS

ILLUSTRATIONS

LOCAL GOVERNMENT

"As time passes, the great local authorities of this country have more and more responsibility thrown upon them through having to cater more and more to fulfil the needs of the people. Nothing is more important than the services of water, cleansing, lighting, electricity, and markets. This is part of a great movement for improving the general well-being and the health of our people. One way to ensure and maintain good health is through clean, wholesome, honest food, and a market like this gives the citizens opportunities of obtaining it."

ARTHUR GREENWOOD, *Minister of Health,* 1930

TOWN GOVERNMENT IN THE SIXTEENTH CENTURY

CHAPTER I

INTRODUCTION

MANY people interested in Local Government must often meditate on the nature of this work in the early days of town history. How was the town governed in the past? What concept had the rulers of their civic office? Did membership of the ruling body imply duties or only privileges, or both? What was their idea of a well-governed town?

These and many other questions suggest themselves to the interested person, but have remained unanswered, for the interest of the town historian seems to have ended with those fifteenth-century developments that gave many towns an oligarchic form of government. The interest lay in tracing the constitutional changes, and when these ceased the constitutional historian saw nothing more of importance to relate. Yet the century that followed was one of the most interesting periods in town life. With the growth of capitalism the old system of subsistence farming was breaking down, and the development of sheep-farming not only prevented the normal expansion of the country dwellers on the land, but actually displaced many of them. In trade, cloth took the place of wool as the chief article of export, and as a result towns that had prospered as centres of the wool trade began to decay. Further, the old methods of production, suitable as they might have been for a limited market, could not serve an expanding international one, and a new type of industrial organization developed.

To the towns, these changes brought almost the same problems that confront the nation-state of the twentieth century. To-day separate countries are trying to solve problems arising from world conditions. For the solution of such problems an international authority is indispensable, yet no such authority exists. In the early sixteenth century the towns were in a similar position. English social and economic development preceded political development by half a century. A national government existed, but it lacked the knowledge and administrative mechanism to govern the country effectively, for the prevention of disorder is but one aspect of government, and the people of the towns would have been in a sad plight if they had waited until the central authority introduced social legislation. The problem of unemployment is one example. Employment no longer depended on local conditions. "Work," said a sixteenth-century writer who had been describing the sufferings of the poor in his town during a period of famine, "was very scant for poor people during this period owing to the War with Flanders." (1)

Faced with social and economic facts, town authorities had yet to operate within prescribed limits, and this should be remembered when examining their attempts to solve the problems that confronted them. If, when dealing with poverty or pestilence, the authorities only regarded the interests of their particular town, it was because they had no control over external causes. If plague was introduced into London by vermin in ships or goods from the East, other town authorities could not prevent the ships arriving or secure the disinfection of the goods. Their only course was to prevent suspected goods or infected people entering their town, and this they tried to do. In dealing with poverty or unemployment the town could not provide for people from the surrounding country-side and cannot be blamed for excluding them. The parochial attitude of the sixteenth-century town rulers still exists in the twentieth; the former excluded the "foreigner," and now, though the area is wider, the foreigner still receives the same treatment.

Within these limits the town authorities did splendid work. Long before the central government took action, the problems of poverty, unemployment, and disease were already examined and remedies adopted. The Elizabethan Poor Law Statutes gave no new ideas to the town, but attempted to organize town practices on a national basis. In every-day matters the town authorities were just as progressive. When every form of private enterprise had failed to provide the citizens with an abundant supply of candles—then the only source of artificial light—the municipal factory was instituted and became the forerunner of the municipal gas or electricity undertaking. The social problems arising out of the ale trade were examined, and regulations made to control quality, measures, licences, hours of opening, and to punish drunkenness. One branch of municipal activity is of special interest. New conditions often placed traders under a disadvantage. Their capital was sufficient for local trade, but not for some of the new demands. People who had supplied the town with wood for fuel were unable to provide coal when this came into general use. The corn badgers could supply the town market from a local area, but when scarcity arose their resources were insufficient to bear the heavy cost of transport. In both cases town authorities had to supply the trader with the necessary capital or provide the goods themselves. Unfortunately in this connection a change in the meaning of the words "poor people" is apt to be misleading as to the nature of this work. When the sixteenth-century town authority made provision for the "poor" it did not mean for paupers. At that time "the poor" were the ordinary working people, and the authorities sometimes found it necessary to provide goods for their use that the private trader could not supply. It should be noted that these goods were not distributed free, but sold at a price that covered the costs and often left a good profit on the transaction. Seen in this light, some of the activities of the authorities must be regarded as examples of successful municipal trading and not as attempts to relieve the poor.

Town sanitation and the treatment of infectious diseases have their special interest. During the sixteenth century outbreaks of diseases were frequent, and though little is known about these diseases, they are generally attributed to the filthy condition of the streets, to impure supplies of water, and to the absence of regulations formed to secure a decent standard of sanitation within the town. But if one asks for definite details nothing certain seems to be known. Leland, a famous sixteenth-century traveller, visited many towns before he reached one where the condition of the streets called for adverse comment, so these may not have been so bad as usually supposed. May it not be that the many references to the condition of the highway across open field and over hill and dale have created the impression that streets and roads were alike? The whole question of town sanitation at the time is so much a matter of conjecture that an attempt has been made to show how the authorities tried to secure clean streets, to obtain pure water, to remove or prevent the existence of things thought to be detrimental to the health of the people, and dealt with the problem of infectious diseases.

But to understand the problem of town government in the sixteenth century it is necessary to realize some of the great differences between towns of that date and those of to-day. Modern towns have their tens or hundreds of thousands of inhabitants living in miles of continuous streets, and their interests are almost entirely industrial or commercial. The sixteenth-century town was very different. Norwich, then one of the largest cities in the country, had a population of about 17,000; in Leicester were 4,000; Cambridge, excluding the 1,500 students, had 4,990 inhabitants; Coventry could boast of "6,601 women, men, and children"; while Liverpool was then a village of some 750 people.

The town was both an agricultural centre and the home of the craftsmen. It was the market for surrounding districts. Its citizens had their "common rights," kept their cattle on the town pastures, and within the city walls gardens occupied a large part of the available space. It must, however, be understood that the working class within the area were not agricultural labourers, nor did they combine agricultural and industrial occupations to gain a livelihood. The towns possessed common lands, but usually only the aristocracy had the "rights of common." Thus at Nottingham, "burgesses" might have eight cattle on the town land, while at Oxford "freemen" could pasture animals on "Portmeadow." Even if there were open commons or some workers paid for the right to graze a cow, this did not constitute an alternative means of livelihood. At Newcastle the coalminers usually kept a cow, but so little was this regarded as a source of profit "that these poor men who worked coal under the ground and had no other means of sustaining their families than their own labour" were justified in demanding higher wages because the rising price of grazing land had increased the cost of keeping the cow. (2) In the sixteenth-century town the workers were wage-earners dependent upon capitalist-controlled industries for their living. Their wives may have earned a little money by spinning or knitting or working as charwomen just as some married women do to-day, but the unemployed gardener, tailor, or blacksmith was a craftsman looking for work at his own craft. Something of this can be seen from the census "of the poor of the Parish of St. Stephens," which is given in the *Norwich Records*, and reproduced at the end of this work.

NOTES

1. *Gloucester, Hist. MSS. Comm. Report* 12. App. Part ix. 459.
2. Welford, *Newcastle and Gateshead*, iii. 62.

CHAPTER II

THE TOWN COUNCIL

DURING the sixteenth century most towns were governed by organized bodies over whom the rest of the citizens had little, if any, control. Usually the Council consisted of two groups, one a body of Aldermen known as the "Mayor's Brethren," or the "Twenty-four," and the other as the "Forty-eight," or "Common Council." The relationship between these two groups might vary from town to town, but together they formed the ruling authority, and only the direct interference of the Crown could affect its decisions.

Whether a town authority originated with a Merchant Gild, developed from a Leet Court, or, as at Norwich, commenced with a group of free citizens, there was the same tendency for it to become oligarchic. The explanation of this must be sought in the social conditions of the time. First, people were not eager to take civic office; so it must not be assumed that town government began with all the citizens being deeply interested, anxious to share in the work, and that later they were deprived of greatly valued rights. Secondly, the privilege of self-government had to be paid for, and some organized group had to be responsible for payment. If the dues were not rendered there would be no complicated law process, the King or other Lord of the Manor would merely seize property belonging to one or more of the wealthy citizens. The natural result was that those who might suffer in case of default were the most interested, and gradually acquired the reins of government.

At first the Lord of the Manor had rights within the town. At the local Courts he or his representative administered justice, and the fines inflicted were one of his sources of revenue. The privilege of holding a market was also his, and rents for stalls and tolls for permission to trade added to his income. His monopoly rights in these and other things may not have been oppressive, but by the inhabitants of a developing town he could only have been regarded as an intruder, and when they decided to buy out these rights and free the town from his officials, the first step towards municipal freedom had been taken. The money value of his privileges was ascertained, and paid to him as a yearly rent, which was usually known as the "Fee-Farm," and in return the town secured the right of self-government. Then the "Town Court" passed under the control of the town authority, and citizens charged with any ordinary offence had the right to be tried in their town by the local Justices of the Peace, while the Leet Court, all-important when the Lord controlled the town, gradually deteriorated into a petty police court. The market rights were transferred to the town, and there the Mayor proclaimed the "Assize of Bread and Ale," the town's authority being so complete that not even the Crown officials could interfere.

The time had now arrived when a Charter was necessary so that the privileges of the town might be legally recorded and safeguarded. The Charter must be purchased from the King, and every change in the monarchy made it necessary to secure a new Charter. No one Charter can be taken as a guide to the development of the town, for in each its rights are stated as if then given for the first time, while in fact they may have been but renewed. Further, in many cases the issue of a new Charter gave the town authorities an opportunity to secure legal sanction for practices that had been long in vogue.

Because of the ease with which a wealthy Gild could buy out the rights of an overlord, it is found that in most towns civic government began with the Merchant Gild. The "Fee-Farm" was secured, the town became a Borough, and the Gild members were the Burgesses and members of the ruling authority. In such a town there may have been others free to trade within the Borough, but the Gildsmen as

B

Burgesses decided the conditions. Northampton secured the "Fee-Farm" of the town in 1189, and Lincoln in 1194, and in each town the Lord's representative was then replaced by a citizen who was known as the Reeve. In 1229 at Oxford, 1247 at Chester, 1251 at Leicester, and 1252 at Northampton, the "Reeve" took the title of "Mayor."

Of early development little is known, but during the fourteenth century town records begin to refer to a governing body called the "Twelve" or the "Twenty-four." These were the "Mayor's Brethren" of a later date. Although referred to in this way, for a long time their number was not rigidly fixed, and there may have been more or less than twelve or twenty-four. It is probable that they were a body of ex-officials—ex-Mayors or Chamberlains—who after their term of office continued to act on behalf of the town. Whatever their origin, during the century they secured almost complete control over town affairs, and their position was strengthened by the fact that, once membership was obtained, they retained it for life. In all probability while the "Twelve" or "Twenty-four" carried on the every-day business of governing the town, other Burgesses were not excluded from the meetings; in fact their presence may have been necessary to ratify the by-laws initiated by the select body. At this stage the town government would be similar to that of a Joint Stock Company to-day, the "Twelve" being the Directors, and the Burgesses the shareholders. During the fifteenth century there were further developments which tended to exclude the Burgesses or Citizens from direct participation in the Council meetings. A new group was introduced which may have been intended to represent the rest of the inhabitants, but was not always subject to their control; in fact in some cases it was controlled entirely by the "Mayor's Brethren." This was the "Forty-eight," or "Common Council," and their relationship to the inhabitants and to the Mayor's Brethren can best be seen from the records of a few towns.

Northampton Council developed from a Merchant Gild. The town was part of the ancient demesne of the Crown, and at the time of the Doomsday survey, the King in addition to his rights as Lord of the Manor owned one hundred houses in the town. These rights were passed to the Earls of Northampton, and, in 1189, when the last of the Earls died, were estimated to be worth £120 yearly. The Gild offered to pay this amount direct to the King and so secured the "Fee-Farm" with control over courts, prison, and market. (1) By the middle of the fourteenth century the "Twelve" had evolved, and by the beginning of the next century had become a "Twenty-four." The Mayor and "Twenty-four" were the governors of the town, although for the election of a Mayor, and for any new developments or disposal of town property, the attendance and sanction of the Burgesses were necessary. (2) In 1459 the Mayor was granted the status of a Justice of the Peace. (3) In 1489 Northampton, by Act of Parliament, was compelled to adopt a new constitution. The Mayor and "Twenty-four" were to elect a second chamber of forty-eight citizens who had not previously held office in the town, and these were to take the place of the Burgesses at the Council meetings. To all intents this body was elected for life, although the "Twenty-four" had power to dismiss any of them for misconduct; the "Twenty-four" and "Forty-eight" were to elect future Mayors. This close corporation was the ruling body during the sixteenth century. (4) The Statute that imposed these changes also applied to Leicester, where developments had been similar to Northampton.

Municipal freedom developed slower and slightly different at Norwich, and this may have been due to the absence of a rich, well-organized Gild. In 1194 the town paid 200 marks for the right to elect a Reeve, and also secured the "Fee-Farm" for £108. In 1223 the Reeve was superseded by four Bailiffs, and as at some earlier period the town had been divided into four large wards and these subdivided into twelve, probably one Bailiff presided over each of the large wards. Complete jurisdiction over the Courts was not gained until 1256, when the town secured as a right that any arrested citizen awaiting trial should not be confined elsewhere than in the town gaol; in those days an important and valued safeguard. By 1347 the "Twenty-four" was established. In 1404 one thousand marks was loaned to the King, and a Charter secured which gave the town the status of a County, and replaced the four Bailiffs by a Mayor, who with four others were to be Justices of the Peace. Ten years later the tenure of office by the "Twenty-four" was made permanent, for it was agreed that once a man had been elected to the "Twenty-four" he should be re-elected annually unless disqualified for some misdemeanour. At the same time a "Common Council" was formed, consisting of sixty citizens elected in wards, "by the free citizen householders." (5) This position was legalized by a Charter in 1417, when the "Twenty-four" became Aldermen, but not connected with a ward. At this period the "Twenty-four" made the by-laws, which, however, had to be confirmed by the Council of sixty, who controlled the affixing of the town seal. The Common Council did not ask for power to initiate legislation, but were satisfied with being able to accept or reject the proposals of the Aldermen. In 1452 the Mayor, Recorder, and all ex-Mayors became Justices of the Peace. The position during the sixteenth century was that the Common Council put forward two names for the office of Mayor, and from these the existing Mayor and the Aldermen ("The Twenty-four") chose one by vote. The Council of "Twenty-four" were life members, but when a vacancy occurred names of successors were submitted to the wards. The members of the Common Council were to be elected by the householders.

How little one can generalize is seen by a perusal of the *Nottingham Records*. In 1448 the ruling body consisted of thirteen persons. Seven of these, including the Mayor, were

Justices of the Peace, and the other six were Aldermen. These probably formed two bodies—the group of Aldermen being known as the Common Council. The Burgesses had the right to attend meetings, and to vote on the proposals of the Council. In 1577 there was an attempt on the part of the Burgesses to make a body of ex-Chamberlains, known as "The Clothing," into a "Forty-eight," but they only succeeded in compelling the Council to increase the number of Common Councillors to twelve. During the latter part of the century the position was that, once elected, both Aldermen and Councillors were life members. The Aldermen had to be selected from the Councillors, and new Councillors from the "Clothing." Both were selected by the Council and not by the Burgesses. The latter, however, retained the right to sanction or reject important measures dealing with the leasing and selling of town property. (6)

The boroughs sent representatives to Parliament, but as the privileges of the town rested on its Charter, the citizens were not greatly interested. The Lincoln scribe states that "the Mayor who is now come from the Parliament sheweth what he and the Recorder have done in Parliament, and there is now owing to them for their expenses £12."(7) Sending men to London at a cost of "four shillings a day" was a burden, so when individuals with more to lose or gain wished to secure favourable representation in Parliament, some towns were willing to allow them to nominate and pay the expenses of particular citizens. When asking Grimsby to elect a certain man as Burgess to Parliament, Sir Francis Ayscogh added "he shall take no fee of you for being Burgess," and at another time their representative, who signed himself "yours yet unacquainted," stated that he "would serve them without charge." (8) Lincoln usually elected two of their own townsmen, but for a Parliament held when they were trying to secure the "Fee-Farm" of the town from the Earl of Rutland, he "for his goodness heretofore and hereafter to be showed" was allowed to nominate one of the members. Many years later a man who "at the request of his nephew" had been made a freeman of the town and one of the representatives at Parliament promised "to attend in Parliament anything beneficial to the City and to pay his own expenses." (9)

If not keenly interested in Parliament the town never forgot that to choose representatives was one of its privileges. The Salisbury Council decided that all representatives should be members of the Council, and in 1592 refused to accept the nominee of an outside person, although an offer was made to defray all parliamentary expenses. (10) In 1555 Gloucester Council decided that only Burgesses should be nominated, and in 1580 told the Earl of Leicester that the Burgesses would never agree to his being allowed to nominate a member.

Members were elected by the Council and not by the whole of the freemen, and at one election at Lincoln the voting is registered in this way. (11)

George Seyntpoll Recorder	29	voices
Thomas Grantham	36	,,
John Broxholme	15	,,
William Yattes	4	,,

By the sixteenth century many towns had so developed that even the "Fee-Farm" payment was irksome, but the *Lincoln Records* show that it was not easy to persuade the person who received the rent to accept a final sum instead of annual payments. Early in the century the "Fee-Farm" rent was shared between Sir Thomas Lovell and the Dean and Chapter of the Cathedral Church, the former claiming £100 and the Church authorities £80. The amount actually paid was not so much, for Lovell had agreed to accept "20 Marks yearly in full payment of the £100." The town authorities were greatly perturbed when his death occurred in 1524, and at a special Council meeting steps were taken to secure the same terms for his successor. From the beginning, the Council appear to have determined to pay no more than formerly, and in 1528 declared that it was impossible to pay more, for Lincoln "had 200 houses clearly decayed and the Sheriffs have not of certainty where they can gather £30 towards their charges," that is toward meeting the general expenditure of the town.

In 1531 their attention was turned to the possibility of securing the advowsons of a number of Church livings and transferring these to the Church authorities in satisfaction of their £80 rent. In 1536 the Earl of Rutland was receiving the portion of the "Fee-Farm" formerly paid to Sir T. Lovell, but was pressing his right to the £100 yearly. He agreed to allow his claim to be tested by arbitration, and was bound in a sum of £2,000 to accept the verdict. If it was so submitted, the result must have favoured the town authorities, for they continued to pay 20 marks. The matter was constantly mentioned, but no further move was made until 1543, when the Recorder and an ex-Mayor were appointed to go to London and petition the King that some benefice should be given to the Cathedral authorities in payment of the £80 rent. In 1544 and 1545 letters from the Duke of Suffolk show that the town's representatives were in London trying to secure the transfer of a Church living, and in the following year the King granted the town the "advowsons of Hanslope, Hemyswell, Surflett and Bentone." For these the town had to pay the King £135, but were not to disturb the present incumbents. For six years prior to this the Council had been trying to secure control over the possessions of the "Great Gild," at first only as a loan, but up to this time "Alderman Yattes," who had charge of the Gild's plate and deeds, had refused to surrender them. The threat of a £20 fine had its effect, and it is recorded that "William Yattes—Graceman to the Gild of St. Mary's, called the Great Gild—with consent of the whole fraternity, brothers and sisters—give for the relief of the city—to the Mayor, Sheriffs, and Commonalty and their successors for ever—

all the lands and tenements of the same Gild, with all the evidence and deeds." (12) More money was raised by dismantling and selling the decayed Trinity Church, and then the Council were prepared to meet the costs of buying out the "Fee-Farm" owners. Nothing further is said as to how the Dean and Chapter were paid, and the Council turn their attention to satisfying the claim of the Duke of Rutland. The negotiations were carried on until 1558, when the Council decided that his demand should be met "either by payment of money or by exchange in lands and parsonage." The same year he was given "the Rectory and Parsonage and Surflett with the advowson" and £300 in exchange for his rent. Fifteen months later the Council found it necessary to make the Duke "a present of two fat oxen that he may be good to acknowledge a recovery of the fine of the 'Fee-Farm' bought of him." A fortnight later the Duke signed the deeds, and the last barrier to complete freedom of the town had been surmounted.

During the century Town Council meetings were developing the many formalities that constitute procedure to-day. In 1500 the Mayor of Coventry was instructed "to keep Council once in the week specially on the Wednesday, and the Mayor's Sergeant shall warn the Mayor's Brethren every Tuesday to be at St. Mary's Hall at the Council on the Wednesday." In most towns formal notice of the Council meetings were given and fines enforced for late or non-attendance. At Chester in 1571 the members were attending so irregularly "that the Mayor many times for want of sufficient number had been forced to break up the meeting without notice of any order being taken." To remedy this it was decided that the Sergeant "shall give notice before seven o'clock the evening before—to the party, his wife, or to a child over nine years of age," and at the beginning of the meeting the names were to be called and absentees fined. At Ipswich the by-laws required that "the Horn and Trumpe must be blown in each ward the night preceding the meeting," and one important meeting had to be abandoned because "there was not time to give a certain Alderman the legal notice." (13) In many towns, as at Oxford, the regulations merely provided that "sufficient notice be given to all members." To leave the Council Chamber before the Mayor departed was thought to show a lack of courtesy, and at Leicester offenders were fined.

How reading the minutes of a previous meeting originated can be seen from the *Records*. At first it was to remind Councillors responsible for administering the by-laws that certain orders had been passed. In 1517 the Coventry authorities decided "that from henceforth, the books of two leets next before shall remain openly on the Shekyr that they may be seen every Wednesday by the Council of the City, to see what is kept and what is broken, and see it reformed; and that they determine these matters afore they enter upon any other." For similar reasons the Leicester Council decided "that once in the year at a Common Hall, the Mayor shall cause the Acts to be perused and examined, to the intent that better reformation may be had." But long before the end of the century the reading of the Minutes must have become general and for the same reason that they are read to-day. At Lincoln the Council decided "that all orders made at the Common Council shall be drawn on paper and read openly at the next Council meeting before they be entered, that if anything be mistaken it may be reformed before it is entered in the Council Book." (14) From the *Oxford Records* may be seen how Councillors were expected to behave in the meeting. "Every man of the Council—excepting Mayors past and present, Aldermen and Justices—speaking in the Council House, shall stand up bare-headed and uncovered, in decent order telling his tale; and whosoever beginneth any talk not then and there standing up bare-headed and uncovered—except those before accepted—shall pay for every so doing, fourpence to be paid forthwith. Anyone interrupting he that telleth his tale to forfeit fourpence, except the Mayor, who may speak to him as he listeth." (15)

It will be seen that by the beginning of the century constitutional growth had ceased. In most of the towns power was vested in groups that acknowledged no outside control, yet the constitution of those groups varied from town to town. The important fact is that within the limits set forth in its charter the town authority was an independent unit with practically the power of a sovereign state.

NOTES

1. *Northampton Records*, i. xvii.
2. *Ibid.*, ii. 17, 16, 18.
3. *Ibid.*, i. 86.
4. *Ibid.*, i. 101.
5. *Norwich Records*, i. pp. xix–lxix.
6. *Nottingham Records*, iv. pp. xii.–xv.
7. *Lincoln, Hist. MSS. Comm. Report* 14, App. Part viii. 31.
8. *Grimsby, Hist. MSS. Comm. Report* 14, App. Part viii. 254–255.
9. *Lincoln, Hist. MSS. Comm. Report* 14, App. Part viii. 47, 74.
10. *Salisbury, Hist. MSS. Comm., Various Collections*, iv. 226, 230.
11. *Lincoln, Hist. MSS. Comm, Report* 14, App. Part vii. 41.
12. *Ibid.*, App. Part viii. 16, 35, 38, 40.
13. Bacon, *Ipswiche*, 224.
14. *Lincoln, Hist. MSS. Comm. Report* 14, App. Part viii. 69.
15. *Oxford Records*, 331.

CHAPTER III

TOWN FINANCE

THE town authorities had no particular system of raising money for civic purposes. Expediency was the governing factor, so methods varied not only from town to town, but in the same town from time to time. The "Chamberlain" was the Borough Treasurer, kept the accounts and produced a balance sheet. The records show that the people were interested in town finance, for one finds requests for audits and recommendations as to the investment of the money. The fees paid for admittance to citizenship provided some of the revenue of the town, and as members could be disfranchised for breaches of the town regulations, the revenue was augmented by fines paid for readmittance. Shrewsbury provides an example of an authority raising a large sum by admitting people to membership. In 1582 the Council decided to pay a yearly salary of £52 to a preacher nominated by them. To secure the money they proposed to raise £300 by admitting people to citizenship, invest this and devote the interest towards the payment of salary, and depend on public subscription for the balance. So readily was the offer of citizenship taken advantage of that in sixteen days eighty people had been admitted on a payment of £5 each, and the £400 was put out on loan at 10 per cent. The Council seem to have been surprised at the ready response, and decided that in future the admittance fee should be £10, but only a few months later, nearly £100 being urgently required to pay for a new charter, twenty additional people were admitted on payment of £5 each.(1)

No system of valuation for rating purposes existed. Lincoln, however, was approaching modern usage when in 1549 the Council decided "that a survey shall be made of all the houses and grounds in every parish—with the yearly rent—and a book to be made thereof," and then went on to discuss the possibility of levying a rate of twopence in the shilling for the support of the parish churches. At Coventry in 1498 "everyone was to be assessed according to the property he held," (2) and at Cambridge in 1598 a levy of 2s. 6d. in the pound was made on all property whether belonging to the town or to individuals." (3) Often the regulations stated that everyone was to "be assessed according to their ability."

At Southampton it is possible that a house tax existed, for in 1550 it was reported that some persons were making two, and in some instances three, houses into one, and the town authorities decided that "every man in these houses should pay as much as would have been paid if the houses had not been engrossed." At Manchester two "myslayers" (assessors) and two "mysgathers" (taxgatherers) were elected at each meeting of the Leet, and these official assessors "with the aid of four citizens" were to levy taxation not only on the citizens, but also on those who having shops within the town, lived beyond its boundaries. In 1515, when Salisbury authorities required £40, they decided to levy all people worth more than £13, and to prevent any injustice, the citizens were to be assessed by eight different persons. The old terms "Scot and Lot" were still used at Ipswich. When money was required, a committee representative of all those who would be taxed was elected to make the assessment. Failure to pay promptly resulted in disfranchisement and a fine, and the defaulters' goods or property might be seized in satisfaction. Thus Robert Baker when disfranchised for neglecting to pay his "Scot and Lot of £8" almost immediately paid the money and a fine of £6. In 1571 the authorities required money to maintain a hospital, and secured it by taxing shipping. Vessels of one hundred tons and over, sailing for a foreign port, had to pay sixpence. Vessels going to Newcastle were taxed fourpence, and those going to London twopence. In return every sailor who had

resided at Ipswich for three years was guaranteed relief if
he should need it.(4) Local taxation of shipping was common, and in 1581 Rye authorities imposed taxation on all
French vessels calling at that port except those trading
directly between Rye and Calais. The following year the
Privy Council notified Rye that because of pirates a war
vessel had been sent to patrol the coast, and the town
must hold itself responsible for feeding the crew and
paying their wages. Their reply was characteristic of
the period. They were too poor to pay the crew, "but if
they can have the prizes they will fit out a vessel or two
themselves."

During the second half of the century the Leicester authorities developed a system whereby the amount of money
required was collected from the "Twenty-four," the "Forty-
eight," and the citizens in equal shares. When in 1559 it
was decided "to have a levy after the manner of a fifteenth,"
the members of the "Twenty-four" were to pay 3s. 4d. and
those of the "Forty-eight" 20 pence each. There chanced
to be only 21 Aldermen at the time, and their contributions
came to £3 10s., as against the "Forty-eight" £4, "and there
was gathered of all the community £31 4s." This was typical
of Leicester's finance, and at no time did the taxes appear
to bear heavily on the Freemen. Near the end of the century
the Earl of Huntingdon tried to secure some alteration in
the method of assessment on the ground that some citizens
were unfairly treated. The Mayor protested vigorously
against any outside interference, and answered that "the
Mayor and Justices do proportion such charges . . . as near
as they can . . . to every man's ability." Nevertheless the
system in vogue was examined, and some of the Councillors
were in favour of all taxation being levied on the inhabitants
in the parishes. Finally it was decided to divide the members
of the "Twenty-four" and of the "Forty-eight" into three
groups according to their wealth, and in a tax levied a little
later the highest-rated members of the "Twenty-four" each

paid £3, while the lowest-rated member of the "Forty-eight" each paid 13s. 4d. (5)

At the beginning of the century Coventry authorities felt that it was desirable to secure resources that would give the town a regular income. Each of the ten wards of the city was asked to select a committee of eight; each committee to meet the Mayor and bring forward any suggestion that it might have to offer. The result was a decision to enclose part of the common land and offer it at a rent to the citizens. Precautions were taken lest the land be permanently alienated from the town, a committee of private citizens being elected to have entire charge of the arrangements. Further, if at any time the Mayor thought it necessary, the tenants had to plough the land and sow it with corn. It was claimed that when used in this way the land served the interests of all, whereas previously only those who could afford to pasture beasts on it had benefited. The advantage of leasing instead of selling public land was clearly realized by the Council, who looked forward to the increasing value of the land adjacent to the town. The scheme worked fairly well, and nearly thirty years later additional land was enclosed and let in a similar way. (6)

The value of town property as a source of revenue can be seen from the Nottingham Chamberlain's accounts. The yearly rents from property and market rights amounted to £74, and at one time when the authorities required £80 this was obtained in exchange for the right to take the hay crop from part of the town meadows for two years. (7) Unfortunately, when extraordinary expenditure had to be met, many authorities found it easier to sell town property than to increase taxation, and during the century much public land and property was disposed of. Leicester Council sold houses and land to meet unforeseen charges, (8) and at Oxford land valued at £251 was sold to pay legal charges arising out of a dispute about Portmeadow, then, as now, the town common. (9) In 1577 the Beverley Council, "for their necessary business, and to defray divers sums of money which otherwise cannot be accomplished," decided "to sell as much of the trees and wood now growing in Westwood as shall be thought good and sufficient." How much was sold is not recorded, but seven years later, at one sale, over one thousand trees were sold.

There was a great number of ruined churches in Lincoln, and from 1533 to 1552 the town must have been largely financed from the sale of these places. The most valuable parts were the roofs and bells, the lead covering of St. Andrew's was valued at £55 and the bells at £10. The stones were used for building purposes or to repair the pavement. Although from 1533 onwards the Council appropriated fourteen churches, it was not until 1549 they secured even the semblance of authority to do so. Then they received permission to unite parishes where the income had fallen below 30s. per year, reserving at least one-third of the income for the deposed incumbents. This, of course, did not give the town authorities power to confiscate money received for the church buildings, and in 1552 the legality of their actions was challenged. The difficulty was overcome by means of a generous bribe, one of the Commissioners being "persuaded to set his hand to a certificate" to the Privy Council "that they may be had and enjoyed to the use of the city without trouble and stint."

Before the end of the century the town authorities were borrowing for commercial transactions, and for some years in succession Ipswich borrowed £600 yearly to finance the municipal corn trade. The credit of the towns stood very high and money was loaned willingly, Leicester borrowing at 8 per cent. in 1594. As security for a loan Canterbury gave two inns, and, as the rents were paid as interests, the Council became tenants of their own property. (10) The security given by the Salisbury Council for certain loans could not have been so tangible, for some uneasiness was felt by the lenders, and the authorities thought it necessary to acknowledge the debts and announced "that at some convenient time the Council shall repay them."

Sometimes town authorities became the custodians or guardians of private money, as when at Leicester Simon Mudd asked the Council to secure him an annuity of £4 and deposited £40 for that purpose. Often the authorities appealed to the citizens to give money for particular schemes, and the latter usually responded generously. For the building of a workhouse at Chester people subscribed from a few shillings to £6 each. (11)

Only one Council seems to have been in a position to act as money-lender. At Oxford, in 1581, Sir Cris. Brome borrowed £80 from the Council, giving a gold chain as security. A year later he redeemed his pledge, but shortly returned to borrow £100 on the same security.

In a few *Records* are items that recall attempts made by the Government to raise money by sweepstakes. To induce people to invest money in one lottery the Government issued the following notice: "A very rich lottery without any blanks, containing a great number of prizes as well as of ready money as of plate, having been priced by Commandment of Her Majesty—by men expert and skilful. And the same lottery is erected by Their Majesties' order, any profit to go to the repair of havens. The number of lots to be 400,000 and no more." (12) This lottery, however, was not a success; the day for drawing was postponed for three months, then for a further three months, and later for two months. Nine months after the original date fixed, the Government announced that as only one-twelfth of the required amount had been subscribed, the prizes would be in proportion.

Many towns hoped to profit, and at Oxford everyone became interested. Two collections were taken, and as every effort was made to induce people to contribute, over £30 was collected "from rich and poor." This money was invested in the lottery in the names of two of the City Aldermen.

Lincoln authorities ventured £7 10s., while Bath risked £1 ; Leicester Council showed a good public spirit, for they decided to place £5 in the lottery, and "that if the same shall happen to be returned to the town with any gain, the same shall wholly be paid to the said stock of the town: but if all or part be lost, then the Council shall make the loss good." The lottery did not enrich any of the towns, for the only reference to a prize is in the *Cambridge Records*: "Town secure a Prize in the lottery value 15d."

NOTES

1. *Shrewsbury, Hist. MSS. Comm. Report* 15, Part x. 22, 23.
2. *Coventry Leet Book,* ii. 593.
3. Cooper, *Cambridge,* ii. 461.
4. Bacon, *Ipswiche,* 251, 255, 260.
5. *Leicester Records,* iii. 94, 423–424, 425.
6. *Coventry Leet Book,* iii. 630, 729, 760.
7. *Nottingham Records,* iii. 366, iv. 119.
8. *Leicester Records,* iii. 241.
9. *Oxford Records,* 232.
10. *Canterbury, Hist. MSS. Comm. Report* ix. Part i. App. 159.
11. Morris, *Chester,* 362.
12. *Oxford Records,* 329.

CHAPTER IV

THE TOWN COUNCILLOR

IT is just as interesting to know something about the people who filled the municipal offices as it is to know what they did. What was their idea of office? Did it bring social prestige, and was it sought for that account, or was it merely an irksome duty to be evaded if possible? The *Records* suggest that then, as now, people differed greatly, and while some would seek office for the social standing conferred, to others this made no appeal. To-day there is this difference, the man who dislikes the publicity that comes with civic service is free to reject it, but in the sixteenth century it was considered the duty of every citizen to undertake his share of public work. At first the burden was light and called for little more than attendance at half-yearly Leet Courts, with some responsibility in between for the enforcement of the town regulations. As the industry and trade of the towns developed, local government became more complex and demanded more attention. Custom called for each to serve in his turn, while growing private interests made more freedom desirable. In 1567 the *Chester Records* stated "that whereas previously no one refused the call to office . . . now it is known that some have come to great riches in the town and do refuse to take on themselves office."

A similar position must have arisen at Coventry many years earlier, for in 1521 the Council found compulsion necessary, and declared "that whereas no man of what degree he be that is elected to office can refuse to serve and no fine is thereon fixed or limited." . . . "It is agreed that if any person be elected to serve he shall pay for refusing to be Mayor—£100, Sheriff 100 marks, Chamberlain £20."

These penalties do not reflect what was thought reasonable for a man to pay to escape office, but the belief that no man ought to be able to escape. When a person refused to serve careful enquiry was made into the cause of his refusal, so when "Roger a Lee" of Coventry refused to act as Chamberlain on the grounds of poverty, his private affairs were investigated, and as it was "right well known that John Pagett would not have married his daughter to a poor man" the Council decided the plea of poverty could not be accepted, and he was fined £20 for "being so obstinate." (1)

Most towns fixed a scale of fines to be paid by those who refused office, and the *Leicester Records* contain many examples of their enforcement. In 1537 Mr. Paris "paid £5 at Marty-mass and £5 at Christmas instead of being Chamberlain." "Nic Carter who refused to be Bailiff deserved to pay his fine of £10 but was released in that he is a man partly perished in his sight . . . and hath given £5 to the Chamber, and promised to pay another if called upon." The Council was troubled over accepting £5 instead of £10, and inserted a minute "that this be no precedent in time to come." To prevent favouritism, the Mayor was made responsible for the enforcement of the fines, and should he fail to do so was liable to a penalty of £6. At Nottingham "Cadman who refused to serve as Alderman" was fined £5, and William Fleming of Oxford paid £7 for a similar offence.

Only in Oxford does there appear to have been competition for places on the Council, and at one time canvassing must have been practised. To end this the authorities announced "that as there had been great labour made by people to obtain the offices of Aldermen and Bailiff," in future those who attempted to secure office in this way would be fined £20, "and the goers about to be punished." At Oxford also the social advantages gained by holding a civic position were so valued that those who paid their fine for refusing to serve claimed the right to take their place in civic functions just as if they had actually been in office. So "Henry Wilmot has paid his fine for refusing office as Alderman, is allowed to take his position in civic processions." This privilege was also extended to his wife, for it was usual for wives of Councillors and officials to take their part in civic displays. The records show that disputes arose as to precedence, "to the enquietude of their husbands as well as the residue of the company," and many Councils had regulations specifying the position each woman should occupy, though often the wives of Councillors were simply ordered "to follow the order of going out one after another —according to the ancientre of their husbands." Liverpool had a very formal arrangement. The Councillors past and present were divided into three groups, with the Mayor, Aldermen, and Bailiff as the heads of each representative group. With the exception of the present office-holders each took his seat in his group according to the length of time that had elapsed since he held office. Thus the present Mayor headed the procession of ex-Mayors, and next to the Mayor came he whose term of office as Mayor "was the most ancient." On completing his year of office the Mayor or Bailiff would take his place at the foot of the procession. The wives of the Councillors were instructed to preserve a similar order, and if in church there was not sufficient room for all "then she whose husband was last in office, to remove to some convenient place." (2) In most towns the wife of a Mayor or Alderman was provided with a scarlet gown by her husband, and at death was paid the same honours, the funeral being attended by the whole Council.

The social aspect of the Mayor's position is well illustrated by the *Records*. He was expected to keep open house during his period of office, and was often paid a salary to enable him to do so. When in 1535 Robert Alanson, a poor but popular man, was elected Mayor of Lincoln, the Council granted him "a tun of wine or £4 to buy it with" . . . "for he has many acquaintances and much resort is likely to put him to great cost." In 1545 the Council decided "to pay the late Mayor the usual allowance, although he and his wife did not use such housekeeping nor wear such apparell as they ought." In 1562 a house was purchased to serve as the Mayor's official residence. During the second half of the century money was falling in value, and this is reflected in complaints about the increasing cost of maintaining the position. "The expenses have grown four times as much in forty years," say the *Chester Records*. In spite of the increasing charges it was thought to reflect on the credit of the town if one of the higher officials failed to live in a manner becoming his high office, and at Ipswich a Bailiff had to pay £5 "for not keeping hospitality according to the custom."

At Leicester the Mayor's salary was increased "from £10 to 20 marks to enable him to meet the increased charges,"(3) and at Oxford a sum of money was allowed the Mayor towards the cost of two half-yearly dinners given by him to the Council. At Exeter ex-Mayors received a pension of 40 marks, and if a member of a town council was reduced to poverty he could depend upon the help of his former associates. At Lincoln Justinian Crome, once a Sheriff of the town, had fallen into poverty and was granted a pension for twenty years, and Thomas Wright, an Alderman, was under similar circumstances granted a life pension. At Norwich a pension was given to the widow of an Alderman, and at Hereford the Council started a public subscription and secured a pension for a man who had been Mayor twenty-four years previously. At Reading money for aiding needy ex-Councillors was secured by each Burgess bequeathing a fixed sum for the purpose.

The officials were expected to maintain a high standard of conduct. A vigorous protest was raised against the Mayor of Canterbury becoming a brewer at the end of his year of office, "other persons after being Mayor had lived like gentlemen." At Beverley the Mayor was not to enter a public-house during his term of office. If the Mayor or an Alderman of Leicester was convicted of any offence, he was to be fined twice the usual penalty. At Chester Alderman Ball was fined

for carrying ale on the Sunday, and later the Mayor was fined
for selling ale and victuals. By a Statute enacted in 1512,
if the Mayor elect was engaged in a victualling trade, then
two persons had to be elected to act in his stead as Clerk
of the Market, and this was done at Leicester in 1595,
"because the Mayor's wife is a brewer." At Coventry no
food-dealers were allowed to sit on the Council. (4)

In a few instances the *Records* relate the dishonest actions
of the officials. In 1512 the Mayor of Nottingham was fined
for taking advantage of his position as Clerk of the Market
to enhance the price of some commodities to his own advantage, and in 1597 certain Aldermen of Newcastle were
charged with cornering the supplies of wheat. In cases of
fraud the authorities prosecuted offenders whatever their
position might be. At Lincoln an Alderman who had em-
bezzled £10 of the town's money had to pay a fine of £5,
and a Mayor of Oxford who owed the town nearly £50
was imprisoned until he promised to repay the amount by
instalments and found someone to stand security for him.
A human story is recorded at Liverpool where one of the
officials could not account for all the money collected. The
Records state that "on finding himself so much short he vexed
and troubled himself so much that the town did ease and
bear with him much, and would have done better to him
but that he would not confess his fault; and because it was
seen of all men that he was not able to discharge all things,
the town pardoned him of all but twenty nobles. His son
in-law—a tanner—lent him hides to make payment, and
then this done, he being sick but eight days, died."

NOTES

1. *Coventry Leet Book*, iii. 676.
2. *Liverpool Records*, 105.
3. *Leicester Records*, iii. 137.
4. *Coventry Leet Book*, iii. 682.

CHAPTER V

THE STREET

FEW things connected with the town are more interesting than the evolution of the street. At first it was only a continuation of the country road along which the town was built, and only gradually did it become an integral part of the town. Originally common ground, the water from adjoining houses saturated it during a storm, and the tread of the people, the passing of the packhorse, ably assisted by the pigs kept by the villagers, often converted it into a quagmire. When almost impassable it was ready for its first improvement, and a causeway, or as it was termed at an earlier time a "causey," was constructed.

The causeway was not at first the footpath portion of the paved street. That is a much later development, for the paved street is essentially a part of the town. Not so the causeway. It was merely a method of raising the road so that traffic, both foot and horse, could pass over wet marshy places, if not with some measure of comfort, at least without serious risk to life. (1) Neither was it confined to the town; the highway might require the causeway more than the town. Leland often referred to the causied road, as, for example, when "leaving Oxford by the south gate" he "travelled by a long causey" that carried the road over the marshy ground to Hinksey. The causied road was not always paved, but when this was so, it resembled the paved Roman road, yet with a narrower surface. Some towns causied the road half a mile before it reached the town, and carried it through and beyond. (2) The paved "causey" ensured a clean and safe passage and made possible other improvements. As the centre of the street was raised it was possible to construct drains down each side, into which the water from the street and from the roofs could be conducted.

In this way town drainage began. Separate paths were constructed from the "causey" to each house, the channel being crossed by a large flat stone. The streets of Chester remained "causied" in this way until late in the sixteenth century. (3)

The next improvement was the paving of the whole street, and the change from a causied to a paved street was the great development that made the road a part of the town. When this was done the causeway was transferred to the sides, the side channels filled in and the whole street paved. To provide for drainage a slight depression was made in the centre of the street, and the channel so formed came to mark the extent of each householder's responsibility for street cleaning and repairs.

The change to paved streets and side causeways marks the beginning of great changes in the town. During the existence of the central causeway little notice had been taken of the exact position of a new building, but with the introduction of side causeways a building-line became a necessity; encroachments became noticeable and sometimes even dangerous, and the people responsible were fined. (4) Also paved streets require cleaning, and as portions of the streets were public property and had to be cleaned by the authorities, the work of public sanitation had begun.

Paving the whole of the streets of a town was a costly business, and it was necessary for the authorities to have power to compel the inhabitants to carry out the work or to pay the cost if done by the town. This was obtained by means of a private Act of Parliament, and some of the towns under notice here had secured it before the sixteenth century.

The Paving Act obtained by Northampton in 1431 gave the authorities power to order the owners of property to pave and keep in repair the streets in front of their houses and adjoining their property, and if they failed to do so the work could be done and the property or the rents

SIXTEENTH-CENTURY CAUSIED ROAD

seized until the costs had been recovered. No property owner was to be compelled to extend his pavement into the street above 30 feet, so it became the duty of the town to pave market squares and similar wide places. Cambridge obtained a Paving Act in 1543, at which time the paving of the town was carried out. This Act gave the authorities power to compel individuals and corporate bodies to pave and keep in repair their portions of the street, and to enforce the gravelling and maintenance of all lanes and places not paved. It also contained a clause which fixed the rate of wages to be paid to the paviors engaged on the work at sixpence a day for day work, and one penny farthing a square yard for piece work.

The inhabitants were seldom asked to bear the whole cost of paving. At an earlier period it was sometimes possible to secure aid from the Crown, and in 1410 Cambridge was granted certain tolls due to the King toward the cost of paving part of the town. So late as 1550, when money was needed to defray the cost of constructing "a free-stone bridge at Sturbridge," the "Fee-Farm rent" of the town was remitted for this purpose.

As it was common for wealthy individuals to bequeath part of their wealth for public purposes, legacies for road maintenance were frequently received. At Cambridge the executors of a man who bequeathed £1,000 for charitable purposes added £600, purchased the Manor of Walpole, and assigned the rents to the repair of the highways "in and about Cambridge." (5) At Chester the Clergy exhorted their parishioners to give money for street repairs, and people came forward with offers of money and materials.

Money and property were often bequeathed for the maintenance of bridges, and the lands of one of the lesser monasteries were given to Nottingham as a source of revenue for the upkeep of the famous Trent Bridge. When orthodox methods failed, the authorities found other ways of raising money, for the accounts of Nottingham record the giving of "twelve pence to the dancers that did gather for a bridge at Clifton." (6)

The work of altering the pavement in the main streets of Chester was begun in 1579, and spread over six or seven years. Watergate was paved first, the two side channels being replaced by a central one, "at the charge of every one before his own door of one penny per yard." It is not stated that any other charges were made, but one inhabitant of this street complained that the work had cost him £4.

Eastgate Street was paved in 1584, and here modern conditions are suggested; the existence of water-pipes makes it desirable to consult with "the workmen of the conduit." Two years later the work was completed by the paving of Bridge Street, where the channel was moved to the middle and the street paved "at the cost of the inhabitants there, and with the aid and help of other citizens and inhabitants."

Usually the pavement was made with cobbles, and streets so paved may still be seen in many old towns; where cobbles were not available the undressed stone of the district was used. Ruined churches sometimes yielded a plentiful supply of good material. Lincoln, where once had been thirty-eight parish churches, (7) was very fortunate in this respect: many of these churches had been closed and the stones from some were used for the city pavement. (8) In paving, the stones were firmly embedded in sand and gravel, forming a firm and dry, if somewhat rough, surface.

Materials for paving market-places and streets recognized as common property were sometimes obtained by means of common labour. This method was always adopted at Leicester, where every householder, when called upon, had "to provide an able-bodied person to work one day to gather sand and stones, and for the carrying of the same." (9) Strict instructions were given that material obtained in this way must only be used for those streets that had to be repaired or paved by the town. From one town came a protest against the rising price of paving-stones, and the individual may have had some difficulty in getting them, for at Ipswich the authorities decided to have a municipal store from which the inhabitants could buy their supplies, and any profits arising were to go to the town funds. Unfortunately an outbreak of plague occurred, so the scheme was not inaugurated.

When the streets were once paved, arrangements had to be made for maintenance. Many small towns retained the services of an official pavior to repair areas for which the town was responsible, but in large towns the practice was dying out. Nottingham retained the office of Common Pavior, and granted this official the right to levy a toll of one dish of oatmeal out of every sackful brought into the market. None of the holders of the office appear to have given satisfaction, often being reported for neglecting their work. (10) In 1553 Bartholemew Chettle was charged at the Leet Court with taking excessive toll and with neglecting the repair of the pavement. "His office is profitable and he does nothing for it," said the Jury. A later occupier of the office so neglected the streets that he was compelled "to work forty days without wages at the repairs," and the Aldermen were instructed to oversee his work. Two years later, in 1579, he was in Court again, and the Jury decided that the toll on oatmeal, which had always been a source of trouble, should be abolished. The Chamberlain's accounts show that women were sometimes employed carrying sand and stones for the paviors, and received fivepence a day, while men were receiving sixpence.

Other towns adopted more efficient methods, for both Ipswich (11) and Leicester had the work done by contract. At the latter an interesting incident occurred: a pavior had undertaken to repair the common streets for £2 6s. 8d., while the town was to supply the necessary stones. During the course of the work he was kept waiting two days for materials, and for these days he claimed, and was granted, payment in addition to the contract price. (12)

Smaller towns still resorted to common labour, and Liverpool adopted this method to secure the repair of the pavement. Every citizen who had a team was to serve with it for half a day when required, and the rest of the householders had to supply a labourer for one day. (13)

The responsibility for the maintenance of the pavement rested on the tenant. Usually the regulations directed the "inhabitants" to "amend the pavement before his house," and the maintenance of the pavement was the duty of the householder as a citizen and not as a property owner. At Manchester every man "had to pave before his own house, or that he is tenant of." At Leicester the Aldermen were directed to see the pavement amended "at the charge of the landlord or tenant," and at Norwich "all manner of persons having houses or grounds adjoining any common street had to cause the same to be repaired," the cost to be borne by the "owner or the tenant."

At first the authorities tried to ensure the maintenance of private streets by fining those who failed to keep their pavement repaired, and the Aldermen or other town officials were made responsible for reporting offenders. Later more direct methods were adopted. At Coventry the "Common Sergeant" was instructed "to make good where neglected and recover the cost by fine or distress." (14) At Norwich the scavenger could employ a man to do the work and recover the costs in a similar manner, (15) while at Ipswich the Bailiff could order someone to do the work and, if necessary, enforce payment by imprisonment. (16)

That the regulations were carried out is shown by proceedings at Norwich in 1559. At the Council meeting the Mayor stated that the streets of Norwich had been so well kept that they maintained the health of the citizens and won the praise of strangers. He then went on to point out that at the present moment there were a number of empty houses in the town, and the pavement in front of these was neglected to the annoyance of the neighbours. It was there-

fore decided to give the owners of the property three months
in which to repair the pavement, and if not done satisfactorily by that time, they were to be fined and the money
secured by distress on their goods.

There appears to have been no difficulty in enforcing the
regulations, for fines were only necessary in isolated cases,
and as the authorities were ever mindful of these as sources
of revenue, there is no reason to suppose that the matter
was neglected. In one instance at Leicester an individual
was fined "10d. for not paving the causey," and some time
later the Mayor was asked to "deal severely with newcomers
and citizens" who were negligent.

The Chester authorities took the responsibility of keeping
the streets repaired. After the reconstruction of the streets
it had been decided that each inhabitant should pay a small
sum each year, and the money so collected used to keep
the streets in good condition. The money acquired in this
way was inadequate, and some years later the Mayor reported that it was impossible to do the work with the sum
collected, and asked that the matter should be reconsidered.
As a result of the discussion a committee was appointed "to
tax and assess the inhabitants—in the sum of £100 or above
for the repair of the highways and streets." (17)

The instructions to the Oxford Aldermen, that they must
oversee the repair of the streets in their ward, and when
a person made his pavement "too high or too low, call upon
him to amend it," draws attention to one of the troubles
that might arise as a result of individual responsibility in
street repairing.

During the sixteenth century carts and wagons came into
more general use, the built-up wheel with its hoop of iron
taking the place of the solid wood one. The damage done
to the pavement by these vehicles caused vigorous protests
against their use. The brewers' carts did the greatest damage,
and it was generally asserted that if these were allowed the
pavement could not be maintained. So in many towns iron-

bound wheels were banned. At Oxford no brewer was "to carry liquor in the City with iron-bound wheels, upon forfeiture of his wheels," and no person was "to draw timber under carts or otherwise on the pavement in any street, under a penalty of five shillings." At Ipswich "carts were to be unshod after Michaelmas next," and fines imposed for taking carts into paved streets. At Manchester carts were blamed for the bad state of the streets, and "after November 20th no cart with iron-shod wheels loaded with muck, dung, daub or corn" was to enter the town. It remained for Southampton in forbidding the use of iron-bound wheels on brewers' carts, "because they spoil the pavement," to add as a second and weighty reason, "that the jolting over the pavement works up the beer and the barrel looks a gallon more than when settled."

The highway adjoining the town had also to be repaired by the town authorities, but the repairs were often of the most simple kind. In deep ruts and swampy places faggots of wood were laid to act as drainage, and earth from the bank filled in to make all level. (18) To "hew it even" was the accepted method of repair.

A visit of the King or Queen, or the passage of some noble through the town, was often the cause of delayed repairs being quickly completed. The Royal Procession was preceded by the official "waymaker," who had to see the streets were cleaned, and the highway levelled, before the coming of the Royal visitors. At Lincoln, Leicester, and Cambridge, great care was taken to have the streets cleaned and strewn with sand before the arrival of Queen Elizabeth, and at Leicester the people were also asked to beautify the front and paint the sides of their houses.

The Bath town *Records* contain an interesting account of how a proposed visit of the Queen quickened the activities of the town authorities. The streets were in a bad state, so the town pavior and a number of other people were hastily sent to the surrounding towns to hire paviors and to bring experts to give advice. The illness of the Queen prevented the Royal visit, and as only the expenses of the messengers appear in the *Records*, probably the work was again postponed. (19)

NOTES

1. Leland, *Itinerary*, ii. 105.
2. *Ibid.*, 96.
3. Morris, *Chester*, 270.
4. *Nottingham Records*, iii. 133.
5. Cooper, *Cambridge*, ii. 420.
6. *Nottingham Records*, iv. 140.
7. Leland, *Itinerary*, i. 32.
8. *Lincoln, Hist. MSS. Comm. Report* 14, App. Part viii. 34, 52, 61.
9. *Leicester Records*, iii. 163.
10. *Nottingham Records*, iii. 309, 356, 364.
11. Bacon, *Ipswiche*, 208.
12. *Leicester Records*, iii. 85.
13. *Liverpool Records*, 92.
14. *Coventry Leet Book*, ii. 568.
15. *Norwich Records*, ii. 141.
16. Bacon, *Ipswiche*, 217.
17. Morris, *Chester*, 271, 273.
18. *Nottingham Records*, iii. 291, and *Hist. MSS. Comm. Report* 9, App. Part i. 153.
19. *Bath Records*, 49.

CHAPTER VI

STREET CLEANING

IT was considered the duty of the inhabitants to sweep and keep clean the portion of the street adjoining their houses or lands, and the authorities adopted by-laws to enforce the carrying out of the work. At Ipswich (1) and Coventry (2) the citizens had every Saturday to clean and sweep the streets before their houses, and were fined for any failure to do so, the Common Sergeant going round the streets at Coventry each Sunday to see that it had been done. Those living near the market-place were instructed to sprinkle the pavement with water in dry weather to lay the dust.

Most towns insisted on weekly sweeping, but at Cambridge all paved streets had to be swept on Wednesday and Saturday. (3) There was a great deal of empty property in some towns, and steps were taken to secure the cleaning of the streets before such places. At Leicester the owners had to arrange for this to be done, (4) while at Norwich the town scavenger could employ persons to do the work and recover the costs from the owners. (5)

The regulations appear to have been carried out. When the plague invaded Norwich in 1579, the native inhabitants made a vigorous protest against the dirty condition of the houses occupied by the Walloons. "The strangers have corrupt houses and the gutters are not swilled with water." Clearly the English part of the town was kept much cleaner. At Oxford people were fined for allowing drains to become stopped, but there is no reason to think that there were many offenders. At Manchester one individual appeared before the Leet Court charged with "not keeping the forefront afore his door clean." The offence seems to have been unusual, and he was warned that a second offence would bring upon him a very heavy penalty.

The problem for the authorities was not the enforcement
of regular cleaning of the streets, but the disposal of rubbish
from both streets and houses. In small towns where gardens
were attached to the houses this was not difficult if care
was taken to prevent any nuisance arising, and this method
was adopted at Manchester under conditions approved by
the Leet Court, one of which was that any rubbish heap
on private land should be enclosed or "paled round." In
larger towns other arrangements had to be made. The usual
practice at the time was to select four or five places outside
the town, fencing or marking these by the erection of long
poles; to these places the people were ordered to carry and
deposit all the rubbish and waste from their houses.

This method of disposal had its disadvantages. First, the
heaps of refuse, if allowed to remain too long, became a
danger to health; secondly, people who lived some distance
away did not carry their refuse to the place assigned, so
any piece of open land became the site of a rubbish heap.
The authorities tried to prevent this by fining offenders. At
Coventry a reward of one shilling was offered to those who
reported the name of any person placing the rubbish in
the churchyards of "Trinity or Saint Michaels," and at
Northampton those who placed refuse elsewhere than on
the common heaps were fined, and one-half of the fine given
to those who detected offenders. At Nottingham when
twenty-eight persons were fined for placing rubbish on
vacant land the owner was also fined for allowing the land
to be unenclosed, and another piece of land was leased
cheaply to the Castle authorities because the inhabitants
were throwing rubbish on it.

Early in the century some town authorities realized that
the best method was to arrange for carters to collect the
rubbish. The Coventry authorities decided that "there be
a cart to carry weekly the filth away," "each Hall door to
pay quarterly one penny, every shop and cottage one half
penny." The carter had to collect his money quarterly and

the constable was instructed to see the work efficiently done. (6) At Norwich in 1517 it was decided to purchase a cart and employ a man to remove street sweepings. This carter was ordered to take street rubbish only, but in the following year a second cart was acquired to collect refuse from the houses, which occupiers were to have ready for collection each week. For the purchase of the first cart £12 had been collected, and for the second £25 was levied on the inhabitants. (7)

The collection and removal of house refuse and street sweepings was adopted by most towns. At Lincoln a carter was appointed to remove the rubbish each week, "every man giving him for his labour as they might agree." This was in 1538; at the beginning of the following century a town official was instructed "to employ sufficient men and carts to carry away the dust and sweeping of houses and streets twice a week." The Oxford scavenger, appointed in 1541, had "to carry away the sweepings of men's houses as well as of the streets," and a rate of one penny a quarter was levied on each householder. There is a great difference between asking carters to do the work, leaving the parties free to make their own terms, and employing a man officially to act as scavenger and paying a weekly or yearly wage, but once the work had been started the regular employment of a man soon followed, as can be seen from the *Ipswich Records.* The constable there had previously employed carters to remove street refuse, and in 1574 carters were selected to serve each ward as required. In the following year a permanent arrangement must have been contemplated, for at the March meeting of the Council it was decided "that Robert Battell be common carter for the carriage of muck." Some of the inhabitants at once objected to paying the assessment for his wages, and from July to December the subject was often discussed at the Council meetings. In the latter month the authorities decided to continue the scheme and to imprison people who refused to pay the tax.

Cambridge (8) and Leicester (9) employed carters as scavengers and the refuse was collected twice a week, the costs being met "by every house being reasonably taxed thereto." At Leicester all the refuse of the town was taken to selected places, so that the tenants of the town lands might use it for enriching the soil. Northampton engaged a town scavenger in 1601 and made an assessment of £13 6s. 8d. for his salary. Nottingham made a similar appointment in the following year, and the man selected for the position had "to be a burgess," "be paid £6 yearly, have two loads of hay for 10/-," and free grazing for his horse on the town pasture. A year later Chester followed this example and a scavenger was appointed, "because it is necessary for the keeping of the streets and lanes clean."

The employment of "scavengers" became the general practice in the towns. Salisbury (10) and Winchester (11) had the street and house refuse collected twice a week; at Berwick-on-Tweed, where the market-place was swept and cleaned at similar intervals, the rubbish of streets and houses was collected weekly. (12) In the regulations for the removal of refuse references are made as to what shall be collected, and just as is done to-day distinction was made between trade and house refuse. (13) The collection only extended to house refuse and street sweepings, and for the removal of other matter the householders were "to pay as they can arrange." (14)

For the efficient and continuous functioning of town by-laws nothing is more essential than a permanent and responsible administrative staff. To some extent this was met in the sixteenth century by the fact that the Town Council was a permanent body, elected for life. Nevertheless attempts were made to improve the administration, and it is very interesting to follow the development in the methods of control of sanitation at Norwich. In 1532, as a result of weeds growing in the water, and because dirt entered from the street channels, the river was stated to be in a "sore decay." The authorities decided that it should be cleaned out yearly. For the work every Justice of the Peace was to find a man for four days, every Alderman one for two days, and the rest of the labour required was to be engaged and paid for by a tax on the inhabitants. The property owners on the banks of the river were made responsible for the cutting of weeds, and "Surveyors" appointed each year to see the work was done. Nothing more is heard for eleven years, but then the river was said to be so obstructed that "after great debate and after many proposals" it was approved "that there shall be made a provision as shall be devised by work-men—with board and posts—to stop the river by the half part, conveying the water by one half, and so carry away the gravel and such like with carts"—to "make the river deeper where shallow places be."

Whatever the immediate results may have been they were not lasting, for in 1552 the whole position was reviewed, and it was decided to form a committee to take over, and be responsible for, the sanitation of the town. The Committee was to consist of twelve men, "ten citizens and two Aldermen," six of whom, one Alderman and five citizens, were to retire each year and others to be elected in their place. Regulations made by this Committee were to have all the force of by-laws and be enforced if necessary by fines or imprisonment. The Committee were also to have control over all money levied and collected for sanitation, including legacies that had been bequeathed for that purpose. The earlier labour contributions of the Justices, Aldermen, and Gild members were commuted for money payments, and after the Chamberlains had added £14 from a special fund, the rest of the money required for the year was to be secured by a rate levied on the inhabitants. Tradesmen such as brewers and tanners, whose trade effluents polluted the river most, were to be taxed at a higher rate. All the money assessed and collected was to be spent the same year on the care of the river and the streets. Finally the Mayor was

made responsible for calling annually a special meeting of
the Town Council, at which the Committee were to give
an account of their activities and present a balance sheet for
the year. (15)

The scheme was a great advance on previous ones, for
besides financing the work, it placed the responsibility
definitely on a public body elected in such a manner as
to ensure continuity of policy. Further, the work was now
to be done by municipal employees, and not left, as the
cleaning of the river had previously been, to the private
individual.

Other and lesser towns may not have needed so elaborate
an organization, but they certainly took care that some body
or individual should see that the by-laws were carried out.
The Aldermen—as at Coventry—were often made responsible each for his own ward, a surveyor was specally
appointed at Manchester, at Northampton a committee of
six were responsible, while at Cambridge a joint Committee,
representing both town and university, were in charge of
the work.

The drainage of the streets was carried into open drains
or "ditches" through which water from a higher level was
conducted. As the danger to health from polluted streams
was becoming better understood, (16) efforts were made to
prevent refuse being washed down and thus fouling them
in that way. Care had to be taken with the ditches, for
they offered an easy means for disposing of rubbish. People
caught throwing filth of any kind into them were to be fined,
and those who carried on offensive trades such as tanning
and brewing were to filter their effluents by means of cess-
pools or "sinkers," and not discharge it into the drains. The
drainage of swine-sties was especially obnoxious, and was
not to be allowed to reach the channels. (17) At Northampton the Chamberlain had to show that he had caused the
ditches and drains to be cleaned every year or forfeit £2,
and his accounts show that many times the inhabitants

worked in common at cleaning them. (18) At Coventry an open ditch or small stream, called the Redditch, served as a sewer, and the authorities took great care to keep this clear, never allowing anyone to cover it or obstruct the passage of the water. So important did they regard its maintenance that the Mayor and a special Committee were deputed to examine it and to make any regulations necessary to remove or prevent nuisances. The River Sherbourne also flowed through the town, and at first the inhabitants living near the river and ditch were made responsible for maintaining the banks and cleaning the beds of the streams, fines being imposed for negligence. They were also given power to seize and bring before the Aldermen any persons whom they caught attempting to dispose of anything in the water.

This method of depending upon individual responsibility was continued for years, and at times the land on the banks was let cheaply to persons who promised to keep the streams clean. Individual responsibility was not the best method for this kind of work, and in 1538 the authorities decided that in future they would be responsible for the care of the river, and the Chamberlain was instructed to arrange for it to be regularly cleaned. (19)

In addition to keeping the streets paved and clean, other precautions of a sanitary nature were taken. Animals straying from the common or turned loose by the inhabitants were often a source of trouble. The pig wandering at large was considered the greatest nuisance, being a danger to health and rendering futile all attempts to keep the streets clean. Everywhere it was the subject of many by-laws. At Manchester a woman was reported by her neighbours to be keeping a pig in her house. The vigorous protests of the people, both on the grounds of cleanliness and of health, led to its removal, and to a by-law forbidding persons to keep a pig unless they had proper accommodation in the rear of their house. Pigs wandering in the street were declared to constitute "an annoyance and grievance whereof divers of the best quality doth justly complain." The owners were requested to engage a "common swineherd" to collect the pigs from the cots in the morning and drive them to "Collyhurst," a common about a mile away. It was also decided to have removed sties that abutted to any street. A few that did not obey the order within the given time had to pay a fine of ten shillings, at that time a penalty that would prove the authorities were in earnest. The method of impounding was also adopted and must have been resented, for a further by-law made it an offence to try to prevent this or "effect a rescue." (20) Manchester was then a very small place, and the keeping of pigs would be a commoner practice there than in the large towns. It is therefore all the more important to notice that in a small village strong measures were taken to remove and prevent nuisances arising from pig-keeping.

Ipswich made many by-laws on the subject, but finding that in spite of all regulations some owners allowed their pigs to roam, it was ordered that all pigs should be marked so that owners of wandering animals could be traced and fined. All pigs found in the streets unmarked were sold at once by the authorities, and the money added to the town funds. At Oxford, any owner of a pig found at large in the street was to be fined, and the "Bailiff" also heavily fined if he neglected to enforce the by-law.

There was moreover a tendency to do more than prevent the pig being a nuisance in the street, for, as already mentioned, Manchester allowed no sties adjoining a street, and at Chester none were allowed in any of the four main streets. The *Coventry Records* show how far some towns were prepared to go in the cause of sanitation. No person was allowed to keep a pig within the city walls, nor in the suburbs "within sixty feet of any highway" or elsewhere if it could be proved a nuisance. (21) From a sanitary point of view slaughter-houses were as undesirable as pig-sties, and for this reason the killing of cattle within some towns was prohibited. In 1538 the Oxford authorities gave a site for the erection of a common slaughter-house outside the town walls, (22) and at Southampton when a butcher was fined for killing cattle within the town, the jury recommended that a common slaughter-house should be built, "and by the town if necessary." (23)

The lighting of the streets is so essentially a part of street development, that no excuse is needed for its appearance here. When the idea originated, safety was the chief consideration. At first the individual had to carry the light, and an old by-law of Northampton, issued in the fourteenth century, makes the reason clear. After stating that a bell would be rung at nine o'clock each night "for the space of one hour lasting" so that those "in the fields may more quickly reach the town," it goes on to order that no one shall be in the street after the ringing of the bell "unless he carry a light and have reasonable excuse." (24) The light betokened an honest man from whom nothing need be feared. Northampton did not adopt street lighting until the middle of the seventeenth century, but then it was for a different reason. "Every householder taxed to the poor was to display a lantern with a candle alighted in it—for the lighting of passengers to and fro in the streets." (25)

The lighting of town streets was almost universal during the sixteenth century, the usual period of lighting being from "All Saints to the Purification of the Virgin Mary," and from five or six o'clock in the evening till eight or nine at night. In almost every instance a clause excludes "such nights as the moon do shine." Nine o'clock was the hour of curfew, when at Leicester the bell warned the loiterer "that none but officers might be abroad."

The obligation to exhibit and maintain a light was a personal one, but those responsible varied from town to town, yet with a tendency for the duty to become universal. At Chester the "Mayor, Sheriff, and all Innkeepers" were "to have at their door a lantern with a candle lighted." (26) Lincoln authorities required "every householder in Bargate, Bailgate, Eastgate, and Newport,—impotent labourers only excepted—to set over their door or window, a lantern with a candle light in it." (27) At Ipswich every "inhabitant (householder) had to keep Lanthorne and candle light." (28)

Coventry in its by-law left something to the judgment of the individual, for after stating that all "Mayors, Sheriffs, Chamberlains, Wardens and those that shall be hereafter and every Innholder," should have a lantern, went on, "and all those that take themselves to be honest commoners." From Cambridge comes a hint of better organization and of growing official responsibility, for lights were to be shown "in all such places and at such charges as are appointed." (29) At Oxford street-lighting was not adopted until 1614. (30)

The *Records* of other towns show how general were the regulations. At Bridgnorth, Berwick-on-Tweed, Canterbury, Rye, and Hereford the by-laws ordered that the streets should be lighted. The regulations were no mere formality. Officials were appointed to see they were carried out, fines were enforced, and at Ipswich and Rye offenders could be sent to prison.

It can be said that the sixteenth century was the period of provincial town development. The town became the shopping centre, the streets became important, and town sanitation began. Mediaeval figures such as the "Pavior" were passing, and the town authority became increasingly responsible for street repairs and cleaning. There is every reason to assume that by the second half of the century a fair measure of sanitation had been achieved.

NOTES

1. Bacon, *Ipswiche*, 216.
2. *Coventry Leet Book*, iii. 584, 652.
3. Cooper, *Cambridge*, ii. 332.
4. *Leicester Records*, iii. 191.
5. *Norwich Records*, ii. 141.
6. *Coventry Leet Book*, ii. 552.
7. *Norwich Records*, ii. 109–110.
8. Cooper, *Cambridge*, ii. 334.
9. *Leicester Records*, iii. 246.
10. *Salisbury, Hist. MSS. Comm. Report on Various Collections*, iv. 223.
11. Bailey, *Winchester*, 108.
12. Scott, *Berwick-on-Tweed*, 303.
13. *Salisbury, Hist. MSS. Comm. Report on Various Collections*, iv. 223.
14. *Oxford Records*, 162.
15. *Norwich Records*, ii. 115, 125, 127, 171.
16. Cooper, *Cambridge*, ii. 321.
17. *Lincoln, Hist. MSS. Comm. Report* 14, App. Part viii. 69.
18. *Northampton Records*, ii. 534–535.
19. *Coventry Leet Book*, iii. 586, 609, 622, 628, 631, 662, 728.
20. *Manchester Records*, ii. 93, 195.
21. *Coventry Leet Book*, iii. 652, 803.
22. *Oxford Records*, 133.
23. *Southampton Leet Records*, ii. 193.
24. *Northampton Records*, i. 253.
25. *Ibid.*, ii. 268.
26. Morris, *Chester*, 275.
27. *Lincoln, Hist. MSS. Comm. Report* 14, App. Part viii. 73.
28. Bacon, *Ipswiche*, 326.
29. Cooper, *Cambridge*, ii. 338.
30. Salter, *Council Acts*, 240.

CHAPTER VII

THE WATER SUPPLY

AT the beginning of the century most towns had wells and springs within the town that provided a great deal of the water required by the people. The quantity available at the various places differed greatly. Coventry, for instance, seems to have suffered from a shortage, while Leicester had a plentiful supply. The Chamberlain's accounts at Leicester show that the wells and springs were cleaned out and cared for at the expense of the town, and incidentally that even at this early period claims for compensation had to be met by the local authorities, for included in the cost of cleaning one of the wells is a sum "paid for marring the garden of the woman who lives in the house at the springs."

However great the supply of water in the town, few places continued to depend upon such sources during the sixteenth century, and arrangements were made for a plentiful supply of pure water to be brought from springs outside the town. Earlier the monasteries had secured good supplies of pure water, and after the dissolution, some of these were made available for the use of the towns. Lincoln was one of the places that benefited in this way. A dispute over the right of the town to use water that formerly had supplied "The House of the Grey-Friars" was settled by arbitration. The town authorities secured the property and water rights, giving in exchange to the late owners a life tenancy of the property and the "Parsonage of Hanslope," the latter being one of a number of "Rectories," or Church livings, given by the King to the town. Some years later the water supply of another religious house was secured by arbitration. (1) Bath also had a supply that had formerly belonged to the Church, and Leland describes how the town authorities paid a yearly visit to the grave of the Bishop who had granted it to the town. (2) Northampton had a supply of fresh water delivered into the town at a very early period, and often enlarged it to meet the growing needs of the people. During the fourteenth century they were served by a conduit which was replaced by a much larger one in 1483, and this again was improved in 1543. In 1554 their accounts show that the expenses of the conduit were kept separate and there was a balance in hand. In 1583 it was again overhauled, £20 being contributed from the town funds, and every "Freeman" found a labourer for three days for the work. From the terms of an engagement of a plumber in 1587, it is clear that water was being supplied at many places in the town by means of taps, but that no houses were supplied separately. Despite these precautions, there was a shortage in the exceptionally dry summer of 1608, and the water was turned off at 10 a.m. until 2 p.m. and 7 p.m. until 6 a.m. To queue up is not modern, for at the turning on of the water "every one was to stand and quietly wait their turn."

There was a serious shortage of water in Coventry at the beginning of the century. The Brewers and Malsters who had been allowed to use the water by paying a special rate were now forbidden to do so, and it became necessary to restrict the hours of supply. An attempt to secure more water by sinking wells in various parts of the town failed to relieve the situation, and in 1507 the authorities decided to face the cost of a supply from outside. A committee was formed in each ward, consisting of an Alderman and "six of the most discreet persons and the most honest"—"to look what every man will give toward the making of the conduit." Some citizens took advantage of the situation and made contributions on condition that they should never be called upon to hold office in the town. One man gave £40, and another six "fowders" of lead, this being worth probably £20 at the time. Thomas Ward, a baker, who desired to be free from the office of Sheriff, gave "ten marks" and had his wish granted. The conduit was made and water was brought by a lead pipe from a distant spring and delivered at two places, the "Bull" and "Cross Cheaping." (3) The work was successful, and the water problem ceased to trouble the "Leet" gathering for one hundred years.

Chester had considerable trouble when installing its water supply. In 1575 the Mayor brought a man from London and the Council decided to employ him for the work. A month later an agreement was made by which "Peter Morris contracts to bring a sufficient and able conduit from that well (St. Giles Well) in leaden pipes—as big and strong as the Mayor appoints—and bring the same to the Cross at the Parish Church, or as near as the Mayor shall decide." What happened at the time is not clear, but ten years later the work had not been completed, and "John Sanderson" undertook to finish it. Sanderson was to cast and lay the lead pipes, and the town find material and workmen. The work was completed in 1584, and it was then found that the spring was inadequate to supply the water needed, a further sum of £100 having to be spent in uniting several springs. A further supply was available at the end of the century, when water was brought from the Dee to a tower built on the wall, and from thence distributed in pipes to the houses of those who were willing to pay for direct service. This, however, was an undertaking by a private individual who had offered the Council five shillings yearly for the right to supply water to the houses. (4) Shrewsbury obtained a supply of water from outside the town in 1570, and certain lands belonging to the town were leased as payment to those who carried out the work. At Leicester in 1557 a man was engaged to provide a supply, but water was not brought into the town until 1586, the Chamberlain then paying "for lime, stone, and brick at the conduit head." Manchester was supplied with water by means of a conduit which in 1570 was said to be very unsatisfactory, and two years later a movement was initiated to raise money to meet the cost of uniting several springs. When a good supply had been obtained and brought to the centre of the town, it was found necessary to appoint an official to keep the place clean and send away the women, who had quickly realized the advantage of washing clothes near so plentiful a supply of clean water. Oxford was supplied with water as the result of the generosity of an individual, who spent over £2,000 on bringing water to the town. The water was piped from "the village of Hinksey to Carfax the centre of the town," where it filled two cisterns, one for the town and the other for the colleges. (5)

The Norwich water supply scheme was completed in 1584 by two London contractors. As was usual, water was brought to a cistern in the centre of the town, and thence pipes were laid to the market, where taps were fitted for the use of the tenants. Both from the main pipes and from the cistern water was piped into the houses at agreed yearly charges. The whole works were the property of the town.

The arrangements for the maintenance of these works and the conditions under which water was supplied are well worth citing. The two persons who as contractors had constructed the works were to remain in charge during their whole lifetime, "or for the life of the longer-lived of the two," and were to receive as payment one-sixth of the yearly rents received for the water supplied by the town. On their part they were to fill the cistern at the "Cross" every twenty-four hours, and to deliver at two periods during the day the agreed amount to the private houses, and during a fire "as much as is required, or is possible." (6)

The beginning of the Ipswich water supply is unfortunately not recorded, and only general references occur until almost the end of the century. The developments during the next few years were of so modern a nature that a few words on them are necessary. In 1614 "the town engaged to bring running water by conduit to Cornhill and so to St. Peter's Church," and "Portman Meadow" was mortgaged for £200 to secure the necessary funds. In the following year the

gathering grounds at "Walsh Lane" were secured on a lease
for one hundred years. For the next few years water was
being conveyed to the houses of those who contracted for
a supply, and in 1623 a waterworks engineer was appointed.
By 1625 it was found necessary to make agreements giving
the town the right to enter on private property to replace
water-pipes. In 1628 there were threats to cut off the supply
of some who had not paid their water rents, and the water
committee was also enquiring as to the possibility of finding
new springs. Finally, in the following year the committee
asked for and obtained the right "to break up three feet
in breadth into the ways and streets of this town, for laying
of pipes and amending them."

The usual method of distribution was to bring the water
direct to a cistern in the centre of the town, and then if
necessary to place in other parts of the town cisterns
supplied from this centre. From these cisterns the inhabitants
usually drew their supplies direct. Over the main cistern,
and sometimes over the others, (7) was built a very ornate
structure always referred to as the "Conduit," which was
regarded with great pride by the inhabitants, and called
at Manchester "our one special ornament." (8) Of the Oxford
conduit Wood has given a most minute description, and
ends his praise by saying "which for usefulness, beauty, and
neatness, is not to be excelled in the three kingdoms." (9)
At Shrewsbury, Robert Probell for £20 offered to cover a
cistern at the end of Fish Street and another at Wylde Cope
—"with free-stone to a pattern of his own showing." As he
was a stranger "and could not find sureties," he was, "for
the payment of his workmen, to take but twenty marks after
(the rate of) thirty-three shillings and four pence a week
until the work is finished, and then to receive the residue,
twenty nobles." (10)

The Chester conduit was to be built "beautifully and
substantially," to bear the arms of the City and of the Earl
of Derby, and of two others. The mason offered to add

free of cost the arms of the Earl of Leicester, if he could also add his own name as donor. Unfortunately he underestimated the cost of workmanship, which he agreed to do for £20, and later had to solicit the town authorities for aid. (11)

The towns mentioned were not alone in their efforts to secure supplies of pure water, for almost every provincial town had water brought from outside the town. The importance attached to water supplies is one of the signs that municipal government was reaching a high standard.

NOTES

1. *Lincoln, Hist. MSS. Comm. Report* 14, App. Part viii. 16.
2. Leland, *Itinerary*, ii. 69.
3. *Coventry, Hist. MSS. Comm. Report* 15, App. Part x. 10.
4. Morris, *Chester*, 282–286.
5. Oxford, *Wood's City of Oxford*, A. Clark, i. 61.
6. *Norwich Records*, ii. 392.
7. Leland, *Itinerary*, i. 53.
8. *Manchester Records*, i. 160.
9. Oxford, *Wood's City of Oxford*, A. Clark, i. 441.
10. *Shrewsbury, Hist. MSS. Comm. Report* 15, App. Part x. 19.
11. Morris, *Chester*, 284.

CHAPTER VIII

THE TOWN MARKET

No one can see the splendid market-house of one of the old towns without realizing how important the market must have been to the people of those days. In southern and western England many of these buildings still exist, monuments of a bygone social and economic life, and Leland describes that at Malmesbury as "a right fair and costly piece of work"—"made all of stone, for poor market folks to standby, when rain cometh." (1) Leicester erected a new Market Hall in 1575 and Shrewsbury in 1596. The Leicester Market Hall was to be built "at a cost of £76 for the stone work alone," while at Shrewsbury Robert Handcocke, "a mason of approved skill and honesty," was recommended as builder, "for they cannot match the man in these parts in science and judgment of workmanship or in plainness and honesty." (2)

Under the arches of the "Cross," as it was called after the name had ceased to be descriptive, the traders stood, and the stalls and pens overflowed into the streets, though in an orderly fashion, for the authorities strictly regulated the position of each group of traders. The rents of the market formed a considerable part of the town's revenue, and in 1500 Nottingham is recorded to have been in receipt of the rents of over one hundred stalls. A room, that usually served as Council Chamber and Court House, was built above the arches that formed the "Cross," so that the market-place was the centre of the entire life of the town.

In the market the Mayor reigned supreme. Here, as "Clerk of the Market" and the representative of the Crown, he declared the "Assize" or price at which controlled goods could be sold, and on him rested the responsibility of maintaining every condition that made for good market.

At the beginning of his term of office he took the oath and swore to "well and faithfully serve the Queen's Majestie in the Office of Clarke of the Market within the borough of —— and without fear, reward or favour, shall execute and exercise the same during the time I shall be Clarke of the Market thereof." (3)

Since the control of prices, quality, and measure was vested in the Mayor, it was essential that an impartial man should be chosen. The laws forbade a "victualler" to act as Clerk of the Market, and as this regulation would have prevented many people from holding the office of Mayor, it was arranged that during a victualler's term of office other people should be responsible for these duties. So at Lincoln "Two persons were elected assistants to the Mayor for the pricing of victuals according to the Statute, because the Mayor himself is a victualler." (4) In some towns even greater precautions were taken. The prices of foodstuffs were discussed at the Council meetings, and if affected traders had been members they might have unduly influenced the regulations. So at Coventry "no butcher or baker, nor no victualler" was eligible for election on the Leet Jury, (5) and at Oxford "no one interested in two victualling trades" was "to hold the office of Chamberlain, even if elected." Further, if the Mayor was a baker, he had to cease business during his year of office. (6)

As it was impossible for the Mayor of a large town to carry out all his duties in person, officials were appointed to act on his behalf. Evidence of this is found at Ipswich, where was elected "a Clerk of the Market to search and sell fish at the Kay and fish market, who shall be sworn to deal indifferently between buyer and seller." (7) At Oxford and Cambridge the Vice-Chancellors of the respective Universities were the Clerks of the Market, and there were continuous disputes between the town and the University authorities. The civic authorities deeply resented the presence of a second body in the town which deprived them of some of their powers at a time when other town authorities were consolidating their privileges. The authorities of Oxford City in two of their many petitions to the Privy Council gave sound reasons against the office being held by the University authorities. "New College and Magdalen and many Colleges likewise, bake their own bread, have stores of meat and cloth—with all household provision of their own—and the town hath no profit with them." Here then was a great trade that, contrary to all common practice, could not be regulated by the town and from which it gained nothing. In a later petition they urged that the University authorities ought not to be Clerks of the Market, "for if they set the price, they will be both buyer and seller." (8) At the same time the Cambridge civic authorities were protesting against the University authorities having control over the "Assize" of Bread and Ale. "At the present time Colleges old and new being rich, do brew and bake for their own houses, and the University officers give less care and vigilance to the Assize, and for rewards and gifts, suffer great misuse." (9) This struggle between the rival bodies continued throughout the sixteenth century, and must have greatly injured both.

The conduct of the Clerk of the Market was very seldom the subject of complaint, but when he was at fault, the Leet Jury did not hesitate to say so. At Nottingham the Mayor was "presented" for selling herring in the market, "being not able when that he is Clerk of the Market," and with excluding others that would have sold "as good stuff to the town, much cheaper."

When some function attracted large numbers of people to the town the difficulties of transport offered the town traders a golden opportunity to increase their prices. An entry in the *Coventry Records* shows that the authorities tried to prevent this. The "Black Monks" held a gathering in the town from Saturday to Wednesday, and in the Council Minute Book the Clerk has recorded "that against their coming, the Mayor sat as Clerk of the Market and made enquiry of the price of all kinds of provisions, and made a book of the same and set it up in the market, . . . like is done when my Lord Prince cometh to the City. . . . And the Aldermen were to make search in all hostileries, that horse-meat and mans-meat be according to the 'Assize.' " (10)

In a corporate town it was the duty of the Mayor, as Clerk of the Market, to see that all weights and measures were correct. A set of these, by which all others could be regulated, was kept in the church or other convenient place, and from them the town authorities made other measures for everyday use. All weights and measures used in the market, whether public or private, were controlled by the Mayor, and the right of inspection was usually conferred by a clause in the town charter. Over those retained by the town as standards for testing the rest, and over all measures outside a chartered town, an official known as the "Clerk of the Queen's Household" had the right of inspection. The town authorities were jealous lest he should in any way infringe their privileges. So when this official visited Norwich to inspect the measures in the market, "the charter was shown to him with the Mayor as Clerk of the Market, so he tried those remaining in the Gildhall, and further he meddled not." (11)

During more than a quarter of a century the national authorities tried to compel Leicester to adopt a particular standard measure. The whole attempt illustrates how difficult it was for them to force regulations on the towns. The Clerk of the Queen's Household visited Leicester in 1579, and announced that there was great dissatisfaction over one of the measures used in the market. "The insatiable greed of our standard strike," as the scribe records. He was invited to test the measures, and the yard measure was found too long. "It had been broken and peasoned again with tin, whereby it is now too long," and the "Strike," made for use in the market, was "too big by a pottle, but is now made fit." The Chamberlain's accounts show that in fines and replacements the visit cost the town nearly £20, and that for "the Strike that was too big by a pottle as he supposed," they had been fined £2 7s. A few years later the official came again, this time "all of a sudden," and with the same complaint over the Strike measure, but the town escaped a penalty, for the Mayor succeeded in "willing him to come another time." Many successive visits failed to secure the desired reform, and in 1600 the Lord High Justice reminded the Mayor that eventually Leicester and other places would have to conform to the national standard.

The Lord of the Manor should have provided weights for use in his market, but the *Manchester Records* show how difficult it was to persuade him to do his duty. Finding that entreaties were of no avail, the Leet Jury determined to levy the inhabitants and purchase weights that would belong to the town. But the traders who should have contributed were no more anxious to have standard weights with which to test their own than the Lord of the Manor had been to provide them, so that seven years passed before the assessment was collected and the weights and scales provided. (12)

In 1588 the Exchequer provided a standard set of weights and measures for each corporate town, and with this the first great step in national regulation can be said to have been taken.

Corn was one of the chief commodities brought into the town, and the authorities made many regulations to confine the sales to the market-place where they might be closely supervised. The Chester regulations stated that corn must not be sold except in the market, and no sale to take place before the ringing of the market bell. Every citizen could then buy for his own use, but there must be only one buyer for each household. After one o'clock the common people could buy until three o'clock.

This regulation, which allowed the bakers to buy before the rest of the people, is almost peculiar to Chester, where perhaps home-baking was not the usual practice of the inhabitants. Both at Liverpool and Manchester the "poor inhabitants" were to be served before the bakers, who often at the first sign of scarcity were ordered to find other sources of supply. The townspeople were to have the market at Coventry until twelve o'clock, after which it was thrown open to all. The regulations usually required the corn-dealer to have all his stock of corn set up in the market before the time of opening, and at Liverpool, a border market, they were to set their sacks side by side—"Lancashire folk on one side, Cheshire on the other."

The authorities were anxious that all corn brought to the market should be sold, and one way of ensuring this was to forbid merchants to leave unsold grain in the town. People were "not to receive any corn into their houses to be set up until another market day," and at Manchester "no corn was to be left in shops or warehouses, but to be carried out of Manchester." Transport was difficult and costly, and by these regulations the authorities hoped to induce the merchants to sell all their corn, even if it was necessary to accept a lower price.

At Liverpool and Chester, where corn arrived in ship-loads, the custom of making "common bargains" still remained. The cargo was offered to the Mayor, and if the Council thought desirable, he was instructed to buy it on behalf of the citizens. At first the Mayor's option held good for forty days, but in 1581 this was reduced to ten, as the longer period tended to drive trade away. A cargo of wheat, barley, and rye was bought as a common bargain in that year, and a committee appointed to measure and allot the same to the inhabitants. Every Alderman was to have a bushel of each, all other councillors one bushel of wheat and one of barley, "and to every commoner a strike of the same that can best be spared." (13)

But bargains were not always made. A cargo of corn was brought to Liverpool, but when the Mayor announced his price, the owner offered the Council "33/4d. to have liberty to have a free market," and this was accepted.

Toward the end of the century a regulation was adopted that virtually ended the common bargain. Any citizen was to be free to purchase up to £10 worth of victuals if the seller paid a fee of four shillings, and up to £20 worth of other goods for a fee of eight shillings. (14)

About the middle of the century there was a general exodus from the towns, and who should be allowed to trade in the town market became an important question. The citizens regarded the retail trade as their special right, and at Hereford threatened to cease paying taxes "if the foreigners" were not excluded. Some towns issued orders that citizens who had removed to houses outside the borough should not trade in the market "except as foreigners," but the authorities did not always accept the traders' point of view. Regulations were made in the interests of the whole people, and in times of scarcity the market was thrown upon to all "toll free." The working of the market regulations can be seen in the control exercised over the bakers and butchers, who in nearly all towns were numerous and well organized. At one time Coventry had forty-three master bakers and Chester had twenty-six, and at the latter place there was said to be two hundred and thirty-six people engaged at the trade. Both the weight and price of bread were regulated by the "Assize of Bread," this being the market price declared by the Mayor, who based it on the price of corn. At Gloucester, as was the custom elsewhere, the Warden of the Bakers waited upon the Mayor each week after the close of the market to receive the "Assize" for the following week.

The bakers were disadvantageously placed for obtaining supplies of flour. When a shortage occurred they were usually blamed and not infrequently excluded from the

market. At Northampton the town bakers had an extensive
trade in the surrounding country districts, and as their
sales were thought to enhance the local price of corn, the
Council decided to regulate the amount they sold, and no
baker was "to carry above two horse-loads of bread out of
the town so long as wheat was above six and eightpence the
quarter, and only one load when the price rose above twelve
shillings." At Norwich, "when grain was sore and grievously
mounted up in price, to the punishment of the poor," the
bakers were ordered "to buy no corn in the market nor
corn that would come eventually into the market," (15)
and at Lincoln, where for five weeks had been no wind to
drive the corn mills, "to the great famishing of the city and
especially of the poor," the bakers were ordered "to speedily
get themselves horses and carts and send their wheat and
other corn to be ground at water mills in the country."
Further, these bakers often had to share the bread market
with the country bakers; but these were also closely regulated. At Coventry no "foreign" baker was allowed to carry
away unsold bread, but obliged to leave it for sale at
appointed houses. (16)

In small villages still existed the "common oven," the
property of the Lord of the Manor. The one at Manchester
was leased to a baker for 6s. 8d. yearly, and the Leet Jury
there "requested all loving neighbours to come and bake
with the said baker, he baking their bread and other
necessaries as he ought to do." (17) But the disadvantage of
the common oven was revealed when the baker at Southampton "changed his times" and the people had their dough
spoiled. As a remedy he was ordered to have his oven ready
at the same hour each day, and to send his boy round to
notify the people.

At times the ruling of the Town Council was challenged
by some well-organized craft. At Chester, in November,
1557, the Mayor announced the "Assize," but the stewards
of the bakers, who thought the price too low, asked for time

MARKET HALL, SHREWSBURY

to consult the members of the craft. Later the assembled bakers decided not to bake bread at the price set, and an organized strike commenced. The Council met to discuss the situation, and the members agreed that the price fixed by the Mayor "was in accordance with the price of corn and sufficient for the bakers to live upon," and the bakers were asked to consider their decision. They refused, and the Council, to break down the resistance, annulled the Charter of the Bakers' Gild.

To obtain the help of the citizens the authorities issued a proclamation explaining the cause of the struggle. "All loving subjects" were told to "bake all they want"—"and it shall be lawful for any of the town as of the country, to bake and sell in the market." This the inhabitants were asked to do "for the common wealth and state of the City." The bakers appealed to the Council of the Marches for redress, and this Court ordered the Mayor to restore the Charter, but refused to interfere with the question of the "Assize," which rested entirely with the Mayor. A day or two later the whole of the bakers were disfranchised.

In August of the following year nine of the twenty-seven bakers petitioned the Mayor for the restoration of their privileges "as they had not been able to use their craft of bakery, or exercise their rights as 'Freemen' since the date of the proclamation." In return they promised to "submit to the Mayor's Assize, and were willing to be bound in reasonable sums for the observance of the Assize in future." So after nine months the struggle ended in a victory for the town authorities.

Nearly thirty years later the bakers again refused to accept the Mayor's "Assize," but conditions had changed, and the authorities at once proclaimed Chester Market free "to all persons, inhabitants or foreigners of whatever degree or calling, to sell all kinds of bread. (18)

The butchers were even more closely regulated than the bakers, for in addition to food they controlled skins and tallow, important raw materials for two other trades. Sometimes the butchers were sufficiently organized to influence town legislation that affected their interests. At Coventry in 1544 they obtained permission to form themselves into a Craft or "Fellowship," a privilege they had lost some time before. Having organized themselves, they at once secured the adoption of a by-law which excluded all other butchers from the market. After two years, butchers from other places were again admitted to trade in the town, but within a short time these must have been again excluded, for in 1550 the inhabitants successfully petitioned the Council to allow the country butchers to trade in the market, and in the following year by similar means secured the abolition of the Butchers' Gild. But the matter did not end there, for the *Records* show that in 1552 the butchers had regained their old privileges, and secured the banishment of their rivals. (19)

In 1530 the butchers of Shrewsbury were in revolt against the town authorities, for the Sheriff was then providing the market with meat, but at Chester in 1570 the butchers went on strike, with results almost fatal to their organization.

Having received many complaints about the town butchers, who had a monopoly of the trade, the Mayor decided to free the market and allow any butcher to sell there. The local butchers protested against this by absenting themselves from the Saturday market, and the people were almost without meat for the week-end. The Mayor was informed, and he ordered that all the butchers should be arrested at once and brought up for examination. During the subsequent discussion he learned that the butchers had held a meeting and decided to "boycott" the market until the country butchers were again excluded. Two days in prison seems to have quelled the spirit of the butchers, for they then petitioned the Mayor "to set them at liberty for the sake of their wives and children," and they were liberated "to see how they behaved." In taking action the Mayor had acted on his own initiative and authority as Clerk of the Market, but at the following Council meeting the members of that body decided to take action, and passed a resolution that "whereas—upon the great want of victuals and because of the abuses of the city butchers, and to reduce the price, the country butchers were admitted to sell their meat during certain hours on market days, and lest so commodious an enterprise should cease since it now rests on the Mayor, it is agreed that the selling by the foreign butchers shall not be put down, restrained, or altered in any manner, except by the whole and open consent of the Assembly, under a penalty of 500 Marks."

The freedom of the market at Chester remained unquestioned for nine years, when the Council, after some discussion, decided to continue an open market. (20)

An interesting incident recorded at Leicester shows that the authorities undertook other duties besides those of regulation, and reveals them acting as mediators between a butcher and his creditors. In a letter to the creditors the Council stated they had received "the petition of one Thomas Green concerning his inability to pay his creditors." "The said Thomas cannot pay them now," but they were asked to attend a meeting "so that the matter can be arranged to a charitable end," and that "they may be satisfied of their just debts and the said Green so delivered, that he may be in convenient time able to pay the same." (21)

In addition to regulating the markets, under certain circumstances town authorities considered it their duty to secure supplies of the more important commodities. This was so with the provision of corn. When the local harvest was good, the market was supplied through the ordinary channels, but when it failed it often happened that no private individual was prepared to take the risk of bringing corn from some other part of the country, or, as was sometimes necessary, to import it from abroad. So the town authorities had to take steps to secure the necessary supplies.

The last quarter of the century was a period of general unrest throughout Europe, and in England this was intensified by a succession of bad harvests. During the worst years the Queen's Privy Council attempted to alleviate the hardships of the people and to prevent subsequent disturbances by closely regulating the price and supply of corn. The *Gloucester Records* show how the town authorities carried out the Privy Council's orders, and how well they understood how far such regulations could be profitably enforced. In 1586 the harvest had been a failure, and "wheat rose higher in price than since Queen Mary came to the throne." The town authorities were informed by the Privy Council that the farmers were taking advantage of the scarcity to demand exorbitant prices, and they were ordered to find how much corn was held in store. The Justices carried out these instructions "and fixed the price of corn at 4/4." "Nevertheless the same was not put in practice lest the market might be abridged"—"yet the Justices attended the market and abated the excessive price of the owners, and kept the same at about 5/- or 5/4 until the new corn came in." "Notwithstanding the Council, corn continued at a high price, and at Christmas orders for searchers were carried out, and these orders were contained in printed books,". . . "but the price increased and continued until harvest, which was as fruitful a harvest as was seen in man's memory, being inned by the middle of August." (22)

The success or failure of the national regulations cannot be judged entirely by their effect on corn prices and supplies, for the knowledge that the authorities were trying to ensure distribution at equitable prices must have had a great effect on the minds of the people, and would go far towards preserving the peace.

Since mere regulation could not increase the supply of the staple article of food, the town authorities had to devote their energies to the problem. Transport was their greatest difficulty, for on land this was so inadequate that, when in

1587 Shrewsbury bought a quantity of corn in Norfolk, it would have taken eight hundred horses over twelve days to transport it to Shrewsbury. At another time corn from the upper reaches of the Severn was taken by boat to towns in North Wales, the long and dangerous journey round the coast being preferable to the much shorter one across the country.

So when the home harvest failed, the difficulties of transport were sufficient to prevent the private trader supplying the market, and town authorities had to undertake the work. In the famine year of 1521 the Bristol Council provided their market with corn from Worcestershire. (23) In 1527 and in 1551 the Norwich Council arranged for a regular supply to be delivered in Norwich twice each week, also supplying the bakers.

The arrangements for the 1551 supply have some interesting features. First, provision was made for the purchase of the corn at the first sign of a poor harvest and long before a shortage actually arose. Secondly, when the corn arrived it was not sold indiscriminately in the market, but rationed among the inhabitants. (24)

For the last ten years of the century the town authorities made continuous purchases, and although the corn was usually sold at less than market prices, huge profits were often made. In 1595 the Shrewsbury Council bought three thousand bushels of corn and sold it in the town at two-thirds the market price, and in the following year purchased a further sixteen hundred bushels. In 1598 the Council bought nearly five thousand bushels in Norfolk, and this was delivered by boats coming up the Severn. Bridgnorth, Chester, and Plymouth bought supplies the same year, and the last town gained £150 on the year's trade.

The Rye town authorities, who often purchased corn in Norfolk, once in a period of great scarcity in their town seized a small ship laden with corn which lay at anchor in their harbour. They afterwards wrote to the Queen's Privy Council for permission to retain it, and at the same time offered the owner the highest market price for the cargo. (25) The Ipswich authorities bought corn regularly, and whenever there were signs of a poor harvest at home a special committee was made responsible for securing supplies elsewhere. In 1592 the Council borrowed £200 for the purchase of corn and afterwards bought £600 worth yearly.

It is interesting to notice that in the years of scarcity rye was the grain usually purchased, and Harrison, in his *Description of England*, says that this was the corn the working people were accustomed to use.

A quotation from Seyer's *Little Red Book of Bristol* will illustrate these municipal operations for better than mere figures. "The scarcity still continuing in 1595, Mr. John Whitson bought in the month of November, by order of the Mayor and Aldermen, 3,000 quarters of Danish rye of Mr. Thomas Offley of London, merchant, at 28/- the quarter, to be delivered here to Mr. Whitson free of all charges before the last day of May 1596 next ensuing. But the said Mayor by procurement of others disliked the bargain, alleging it to be too dear in regard that it would be so long before the rye would come. Whereby the Mayor and Aldermen would pay but half the charges and expenses that Mr. Whitson had laid out, which was £8 2s. 6d. in riding to London in and about the business, so that Mr. Whitson was to stand one-half the charges and to one-half the bargain himself. But it so fell out that when the said rye was arrived at Bristol it was well worth 44/- a quarter or more. And the said Mayor and Aldermen entreated to have the whole bargain and would pay Mr. Whitson £50 for his charges and running the adventure, whereto after persuasions he— being of a good nature—consented. And within twenty days after, the rye was all sold at 6/- the bushel, much under the rate of the markets, and many pecks and half-bushels were given to the poor of the City. And in conclusion there was gained upon this bargain £774, all charges and petty charges being deducted." (26)

So, to the town authority, the market was not merely a source of revenue. The idea of a just price for a good article still obtained. There were no signs of belief that free competition would work out to the good of all; rather that the traders should be controlled, and when they failed then the town authority should provide for the people.

NOTES

1. Leland's *Itinerary*, ii. 53.
2. *Shrewsbury, Hist. MSS. Comm. Report* 15, App. Part x. 60.
3. Guilding's *Reading*, i. 265.
4. *Lincoln, Hist. MSS. Comm. Report* 14, App. Part viii. 77.
5. *Coventry Leet Book*, iii. 682.
6. *Oxford Records*, 150.
7. Bacon's *Ipswiche*, 227.
8. *Oxford Records*, 113, 123.
9. Cooper's *Cambridge*, i. 348.
10. *Coventry Leet Book*, iii. 589.
11. *Norwich Records*, ii. 177.
12. *Manchester Records*, i. 154, ii. 72, 154.
13. Morris, *Chester*, 391.
14. *Liverpool Records*, i. 82–83.
15. *Norwich Records*, ii. 116.
16. *Coventry Leet Book*, iii. 717.
17. *Manchester Records*, i. 55, 221.
18. Morris, *Chester*, 418–419, 421.
19. *Coventry Leet Book*, iii. 779–803.
20. Morris, *Chester*, 438, 441–442.
21. *Leicester Records*, iii. 257.
22. *Gloucester, Hist. MSS. Comm. Report* 12, App. Part ix. 458–459.
23. Seyer's *Bristol*, ii. 213.
24. *Norwich Records*, ii. 126–127, 163.
25. *Rye, Hist. MSS. Comm. Report* 13. App. Part iv. 114.
26. Seyer's *Bristol*, ii. 254.

CHAPTER IX

THE ALE TRADE

IN the sixteenth century the ale trade was an important industry, and there were many brewers in every town. Coventry, in 1520, had sixty-eight brewers using one hundred and forty quarters of malt weekly and producing seven thousand gallons of ale. The report giving these particulars adds that there were "three thousand, three hundred, five scores and five quarters of malt in stock."

Ale was the common drink, and one clergyman mentions that his wife brewed two hundred gallons every month. (1) Many people brewed at home, so some of the brewers must have been in a small way of business, but the general idea is erroneous that all production in the sixteenth century was carried on by small masters employing perhaps a journeyman and one or two apprentices. In all industries were businesses conducted on a large scale, and brewing was no exception, for in 1587 one Leicester brewer was able to supply two thousand five hundred gallons of ale each week, and two others could each deliver one thousand gallons.

Some of the leading citizens were brewers and the business must have been profitable, for it was said that many were able to retire on wealth accumulated from it. Fortunately, at Exeter a brewer's balance sheet has been preserved, and a study of its particulars reveals the profitable nature of this trade.

Feb. 1556. Confession of Nicholas Roughe, Brewer, of the gains he hath clear at every brewing.

At every brewing	£	s.	d,
6 quarters of olter malt amounting to 48 bushels at 13d. the bushel	1	16	0
8 bushels of barley malt at 2/- bushel	0	16	0
6 bushels of roast malt at 4/- bushel	1	4	0

Of this he brewed	£	s.	d,
20 bushels of the best at 6/8	6	13	4
11 bushels of the middle at	1	16	8
Allow for malt	3	16	8
To wood		14	0

And he declares the remainder at £3 over and above his small ale and grains.

The figures are not correct, but it should be noted that when corrected they bear out the statement of the brewer. (2)

The authorities tried to ensure that pure ale of a suitable strength should be sold, correctly measured, at a fair price. The quality of the ale was tested by tasting. Two or more persons in each ward were appointed "ale-tasters," "to be ready at all times . . . when any brewer shall send for them to go and taste their ale and see that it is able." At Leicester this was the duty of the Alderman of the Ward, who with two members of the Council had to taste of every brew before any was sold. If an Alderman chanced to be a brewer, the Alderman of an adjoining ward acted in his stead. At first only ale was brewed, and this from malt of barley or oats. But during the sixteenth century hops were introduced into England, and with their use in brewing the distinction between ale and beer appeared. The addition of hops produced a liquor that would keep much longer than ale without turning sour, (3) but at first the authorities regarded this as adulteration, and at Coventry in 1522, and at Leicester in the following year, brewers were forbidden to use hops.

The wholesale and retail price of ale depended upon the cost of barley or malt, and was determined by the Mayor. This adjustment was known as the "Assize of Ale," and if properly made fixed both the price and the quality. An old Assize Order of Colchester reads: "Twelve pence highering or twelve pence lowering in the price of malt, always a shilling to the farthing. When he (the brewer) buys a quarter of malt for two shillings, then to sell a gallon of best ale for two farthings, and to make forty-eight gallons from one quarter of malt." (4)

This formula was not strictly adhered to, and often the authorities fixed what they thought to be a fair price. At Coventry in 1521—a year of great scarcity—the Council ordered that when "malt was a Noble or above in price," fourteen gallons of ale were to be sold for not above twenty pence, "when the price of malt fell below a Noble," then fourteen gallons were to be sold for eighteenpence. Retailers were to sell at twopence a gallon.

There seems to have been little cause for complaint, but if the price of malt rose very high, as it did in some seasons, trouble would probably arise. This happened at Cambridge in 1550. The price of malt stood at two shillings the quarter for a few years, and then as the result of a bad harvest rose to nine shillings. The brewers refused to brew ale at the price fixed, and demanded the full statute price. The Council pointed out to the brewers that they had enjoyed for some time a price higher than statute price, and now must be prepared to make some sacrifice. As imprisonment was the alternative the brewers' opposition collapsed.

The lack of transport facilities prevented the quick and cheap transport of corn, and because of this the price of ale varied with the result of the local harvest. This is seen in the price at different places at the same time, and in the same place at different times. In 1553 twelve gallons of ale sold for one-and-threepence at Leicester and for three shillings at Coventry. At Leicester in 1510 twelve gallons sold for one shilling, for two shillings and sixpence in 1521, and for one shilling in 1553.

There appears to have been sufficient elasticity in the manipulation of the "Assize" to allow it to work smoothly. At Coventry changes in the price of ale followed closely any change in the price of malt. In 1552 the price was set at two shillings for fourteen gallons, but immediately afterwards malt fell in price, and ale was reduced to one shilling and eightpence. The fall in price proved to be only temporary, and the price of ale was again fixed at two shillings in accordance with the rising price of malt. At Salisbury the brewers complained that profitable brewing was impossible at the price fixed, so this was increased, but as malt fell in price shortly after, the concession was immediately withdrawn.

When malt was scarce and dear, brewers sometimes tried to escape the unprofitable times by ceasing to brew. The authorities met this policy with heavy penalties. At Coventry any brewer who ceased to brew when malt was dear had to pay a fine of £5; (5) for a like offence at Salisbury, £10; and at Oxford fines for this had to be paid before the brewer could restart business. At Leicester in times of dear malt the authorities arranged that ale should be available for the poor, and brewers were ordered to "brew good wholesome ale for poor people at one halfpenny a gallon,". . ."anyone finding themselves agrieved with the same to see the Mayor and they shall have remedy." Retailers were also regulated. A lower price had to be charged for ale that was sold to be consumed "off" the premises, and they were "not to refuse to serve any man out of their houses." Further, however small the quantity demanded, it had to be sold at the gallon rate, and in times of scarcity there was to be no favouritism. At Manchester "no one was to be denied ale—provided they can pay for it," and at Gloucester every alewife was directed "to serve rich and poor while she has in her home six gallons." Having fixed the price and quality of the ale, the authorities then enforced the use of sealed measures. Brewers were compelled to give thirteen, and in some towns fourteen, gallons for twelve, and the *Records* illustrate the efforts made to check the deliveries. Ale was delivered in open vats, and the jolting of the cart over the cobbled pavement was said "to work up the ale in the barrels and it looks a gallon more than when settled." So at Gloucester the brewers were ordered "to make their cowlys as they carrieth their ale unto their customers, as may contain thirteen gallons of clear ale, and at the uttermost part of thirteen gallons to have a hole with a pin, so that clear ale may run out at the said hole." This served its purpose for some time, but it had one obvious defect, and later the authorities issued additional instructions which appear to have been successful. The retailer was to have by his door "a stone upright levelled," and on this stone the open barrel had to be placed for inspection before the innkeeper accepted delivery. The brewer was expected to deliver true measure at this stone, any deficiency having to be allowed for in the price or by making the measure good. (6)

In the ale-houses both wood and pewter measures were in use and had to bear the official seal of the town. At Coventry the "sergeant" was instructed to seize and break all measures that had not the City seal affixed. At Nottingham every innkeeper had "to have a pint and quart pot of pewter to measure their ale," and at Oxford "every ale-seller was to have four quart and four pint pots, these to be taken to St. Mary's Church to be sealed." Ipswich authorities supplied measures bearing the official stamp, and allowed no others to be used. Leicester innkeepers had to supply all ale in officially stamped pewter measures, but could provide their customers with small drinking-glasses. Similar regulations were enforced at Chester. "Stone pots" were condemned by the Southampton authorities because it was almost impossible to stamp or seal them.

The use of sealed measures was enforced with difficulty for the Leicester man who declared "that the Mayor nor his breder (brethren) should set no syse on his pot, nor the King norther," was not the type of individual to accept new conditions quietly. Innkeepers fined for evasion of the law at Leicester lost their licence at the third conviction, while the customer was liable to a penalty if he accepted ale in an unstamped measure. Sometimes a single refractory individual had to be dealt with, as when "Helen Attewell was presented" at Nottingham "because she would not keep the order." At other times there were wholesale attempts at evasion, and at Chester an attempt was made to escape the regulations by counterfeiting the town seal.

From early times ale-houses had usually been managed by women, and in old stories the "Alewife" is an oft-mentioned character. But with the development of the town, and other great social changes of the sixteenth century, the ale-house took a new aspect, and for many reasons it became undesirable that women should be in charge of these places. It is not easy to say how far the change had gone, but in 1540 a proclamation at Chester stated that "Whereas all the taverns and ale-houses of this town have and used to be kept by young women, otherwise than is used in any other place in this realm. . . . Whereby all strangers resorting hereto marvel. . . . It is ordered that after the 10th day of June, there shall be no taverns kept in this City by any woman between fourteen and forty years of age." For how long this particular order was enforced is not revealed by the *Records*, but nearly thirty years later ale-house-keepers were "bound" to keep no woman "to retail ale or beer,— except it be his wife or daughter."

There were many forces that would tend to bring about the changed attitude. In particular, the drastic regulations enforced by town authorities would make it desirable that a man should be in charge, and the rising tide of puritanism would move opinion in the same way. Moreover, unemployment was rife, and it was thought undesirable that women should do work that might be done by men, and both the national and town authorities tried to force women into domestic service. "There are in this town," said the Southampton Leet Jury, "dyvers young women and maidens that keep themselves out of service, and work for themselves in dyvers men's houses which we desire to see reformed." (7) Economic motives may therefore have been as potent as moral ones in the substitution of men for women as ale-house-keepers, and at Manchester it was said that "single women at their own hands do brew and bake and use other trades to the great hurt of other inhabitants having wives and children." The Leet Jury decided that this competition must cease. In future no unmarried woman was to have a room or house of her own, and after six months "no single woman shall sell any ale, bread, or other commodity to the hurt of the poor inhabitants." (8)

The "Alewife" maintained her position in the western counties longer than elsewhere, and until the second half of the century she is often referred to in the *Records* of Gloucester, Hereford, and Coventry. At Nottingham appears to have been no change, and alewives were still mentioned in the following century.

At first, town authorities attempted to regulate the production and sale of ale in the same manner as other commodities, but as the century advanced they realized that the social consequences of the industry made special regulations necessary. So new methods of control were devised, and the regulations then enforced are of great interest as they introduced all the essential ideas on this subject that are embodied in modern legislation.

The earliest method of control was the "bond." Every person engaged in certain trades had to provide surety for some fixed sum as a pledge for the proper conduct of the business. The custom varied. In some towns a trader had to be "bound" before starting business, and in others no bond seems to have been insisted on, until for some breach of the regulations the trader appeared in the Town Court. Again, some few towns compelled certain traders to attend the Court every year to renew their bonds. At Nottingham every innkeeper had to provide a bond of 100s., a sum equal to £60 to-day. At Lincoln two sureties were required, and for a woman trader a man had to be "bound." The bond provided some guarantee that the regulations would be carried out, but gave the authorities no control over the

number of people engaged in a particular trade; in the
selling of ale, where not only the character of the individuals
is important, but where control over numbers is essential,
the bond was not sufficient. So in 1544 the authorities of
Coventry decided that as a means of controlling the trade
the Mayor and other Justices of the Peace should issue
"permits" or "licences" to all persons who were allowed to
brew or sell ale, and unlicenced traders were to be heavily
fined. At first this only applied to those within the City
wall, but two years later the regulations were extended to
the suburbs. Although this gave the authorities increased
control, it did not secure the desired result, and in 1547 the
Council decided to reorganize the whole trade. A list was
made of all ale-houses with the names of the occupiers, and
a Committee of Aldermen appointed to go through it and
decide how many and which places should be allowed to
continue trading. Afterwards, no new inns or ale-houses
could be opened without a licence from the Mayor. (9) In
this way control was established by the town authorities.
Seven years later the first national licensing Act was placed
on the Statute Book. (10)

The change was drastic, for there is a great difference
between providing "surety" for the proper management of
a business and having to secure permission to enter it.
Further, the licence was usually in addition to the bond,
and not a substitute for it. Lincoln enforced licences in 1553,
Ipswich in 1579, Oxford in 1578, Manchester in 1579.
Some towns reduced the number of ale-houses at the time
of adopting licensing, the Manchester authority expressing
the opinion that "thirty inns and ale-houses be sufficient
for Manchester."

An illustration from the *Norwich Records* will serve to
show that regulations were strictly enforced. In the Town
Court two men were charged with being on licensed premises
at ten o'clock, this being after closing hours. One month
later, at the same Court, the innkeeper was tried and her

licence to "sell bread, ale, or beer" taken away, "because she did harbour the servants of —— at an unlawful hour contrary to her bond." (11)

Sunday closing regulations were also developed during the sixteenth century. At first these were part of the general regulations applied to victualling trade, but ale-houses were soon made the subject of special legislation, almost universal in its application. At Coventry in 1539 an order was issued that no inn or ale-house-keeper should permit "any person or persons of this City, to sit or be in their houses at Breakfasts, High Mass, or Even Song, on Sundays or Holidays." At Leicester an order of the Council, passed in 1578, forbade any person to remain in an ale-house "in the time of sermons, that is between eight and eleven in the morning, or at any time of service or lesson." A Liverpool by-law of 1592 prohibited "tippling or drinking in any tavern or ale-house at the time of morning prayer or service, upon the Sabbath." In these regulations usually one reservation provided that the "stranger" or "traveller" should be free from the restriction, a custom which prevailed, under certain conditions, to the twentieth century.

A distinction was made between inns and ale-houses on the ground that inns provided food and lodging. As the line of demarcation had to be drawn somewhere, the Manchester authorities drew it between those who could "provide two honest beds" and those who could not, and the former were "to put out of their window or other convenient place 'the sign of a hand painted.' " (12)

Very little appears in the town *Records* with regard to inn signs, but their use seems to have been enforced. At the Manchester Court four persons were ordered to exhibit signs by a certain day or pay fines varying from 10s. to 40s., while at Leicester in 1570 the Council passed a resolution that every victualler should be compelled "to display a lawful sign."

Innkeepers had one great advantage over the common

ale-seller or tippler, for by statute they were allowed to
brew the ale required by their customers, and were thus
following two occupations. This was greatly disliked by
town authorities, for at one time those engaged in two
victualling trades at Oxford had been compelled to relinquish
one under a penalty of £10, "for many Cities do decay by
allowing to the contrary, so that there be few rich men and
many poor ones." (13) Apart from this concession to innkeepers, local authorities made every effort to keep separate
the brewing and the retailing sections of the trade. In nearly
every town brewers were forbidden to sell retail, and retailers
were not allowed to brew. At Gloucester the authorities
tried to convince the brewers that in their own interests it
were wiser not to sell retail. "If they sold retail then ale-
houses would disappear; when ale-houses disappeared
people would commence brewing at home, . . . to the
extinction of the brewer."

At Oxford, in 1525, the brewers complained that from
various causes, of which overcrowding was one, "the trade
was undone and decayed." They therefore put forward a
scheme for the restoration of the craft, and as this was
sanctioned by the authorities and so became a by-law, it
serves to illustrate the general belief of the time—that trade
should be organized and regulated. The scheme provided
that those already engaged in the trade were to be allowed
to continue, but no other person could commence brewing
until the number of original brewers fell below sixteen, as
this number was thought sufficient to supply the town.
The widow of a brewer could carry on his business, but only
so long as she remained a widow. When it became necessary
to admit a fresh owner, the sons of brewers were to have
preference, but until that time, the death of a brewer and
his widow meant the extinction of the business.

Just before the middle of the century, at Council meetings,
the authorities began to discuss the social problems caused
by immoderate drinking, and in nearly every town restrictive

legislation, at first of a class character, was enacted. That people should sit drinking in ale-houses was a social phenomenon that disturbed town authorities, and they never ceased to hope that it might be overcome by legislation. In these attempts Coventry took the lead. After reducing the number of ale-houses, the Council passed the following resolution: "As for-as-much as it is daily seen that they that be of the poorer sort do sit all day in the ale-houses drinking and playing at the cards and tables, and spend all they can get prodigally upon themselves to the highest displeasure of God, and to their own impoverishment, whereas if it was spent in their own houses their wives and children should have part thereof. It is therefore ordained—That no labourer, journeyman, or apprentice, upon any working day, shall from henceforth resort to any Inn, Tavern, or ale-house upon pain of imprisonment by the space of one day and one night."

In 1553 these regulations were extended to all inhabitants of the town, and no person was allowed to eat or drink in an ale-house, "unless it be market day and with a stranger." (14)

The town authorities failed to realize that as a result of great economic changes a new social life was developing. In the towns a working class had come into existence, and in general social life was becoming more intense. Drunkenness may not have been common or even increasing, for Harrison says that although poor "husbandmen do get drunk sometimes—how be it they take it generally as no small disgrace if they happen to be cuphotten, so that it is a grief unto them." (15) The restrictive legislation was not primarily directed against ale-drinking, but against gathering in the ale-house, and was due not so much to the growth of puritanism as to the failure of the rulers to understand the social changes. The Gloucester authorities published an almost similar statement to that issued at Coventry, but instead of forbidding working men to visit an ale-house, a

cure was attempted by making it unnecessary for them to
go inside. Retailers were commanded to supply ale by the
"Pint, Quart or Gallon at all times, and at the prices fixed
by the Council, to all who wished to take it away with them."

Lincoln authorities tried to end that practice of drinking
in ale-houses by thoroughly reorganizing the whole trade.
Only "the most meet inhabitants" were to be allowed to
continue in the trade, and each ale-seller was to be assigned
to a particular brewer for his supplies. The retailers were to
sell "out" any quantity of ale demanded, at the fixed price,
and allow none to be drunk on their premises. Although
re-enacted in the following year, the regulations were not a
success, and in 1569 the easier method of prohibition was
adopted. "No person under the degree of a Chamberlain
(in practice all working men) was to be or remain in any ale-
house on any working day."

The Chester Council did not believe that town authorities
could compel all the inhabitants to cease visiting inns and
ale-houses, but they had control over their officials, who
with their servants were forbidden to "visit any place where
ale was sold, to drink or tipple." At Ipswich regular visits
were paid to ale-houses to discover who frequented these
places, although the initiation of this practice called forth a
vigorous protest on the grounds that "action was no more
necessary now, than in time past, when there were as wise
men as now." (16) Northampton authorities did not attempt
any great reform, resting satisfied with the passing of a
resolution "that no person . . . shall hereafter be a common
goer to the ale-house."

The long-continued efforts of the authorities to prevent
the ale-house developing into a social centre are illustrated
by the *Leicester Records*. In 1563 it was stated at the Council
meeting that many men were spending in ale-houses money
that ought to be spent at home, and a by-law was passed
that "no inhabitant having a house" shall drink in an ale-
house. If caught breaking this law, the customer was to be

fined 1s. and the innkeeper 3s. 4d. for each offence. "But," the order proceeded, "if anyone will drink ale, let him have it at home and there drink and tipple one neighbour with another." Some of the Councillors would have been more severe, for a rough draft of this by-law exists in which one hour is suggested as the time one might drink with a neighbour.

Having forbidden drinking in public, the Council proposed to seek into the character of those who were neglecting their homes. If the enquiry was held, the result has not been preserved. The next by-law was passed in 1578. This allowed people to drink in ale-houses, provided they did not remain more than one hour. In 1583, the hour of Curfew—9 p.m.—was adopted as the closing hour, and "townsmen had not to be allowed to stay after it had rung." Fifteen years later the authorities reverted to an earlier attitude, and ale-sellers were forbidden to allow any citizen to drink in the ale-house, unless accompanied by a stranger, —presumably resorting there on business.

In a few towns the authorities turned their attention to reforming the individual. Kendal was one of these places. At the Council meeting it was stated that some men were drinking "without regard to the waste of their wealth, or the misery of their families," and the Aldermen were given power to "send such persons to the common dungeon to reform them." (17) At Manchester methods of a similar character were employed. Any person found drunk had to be imprisoned all night and pay a fine of sixpence when released in the morning. If unable to pay the fine, the man who had supplied the ale had to pay it instead. Further, any ale-house-keeper found drunk had to be imprisoned for the night and his licence was withdrawn. When these regulations had been in force two years, the authorities confessed that they had not achieved all that had been desired, but "the constables were to continue doing their best." (18)

Two other *Records* throw an interesting light on other

aspects of the drink trade. At Chester, in 1582, the Mayor announced in the Council Chamber that "a well-wisher of the City" had offered the Council £100 toward starting relief work for the poor, providing the Council would agree to certain conditions. These were, that the number of ale-houses should be reduced and no citizen be allowed to drink in one, that the price of ale be never above twopence a gallon, and that the poor be provided with work and com-pelled to labour or leave the town. The offer was con-sidered but not accepted, for the Council felt "that the conditions were unnecessary, and in fact such as could not be enforced."

The second *Record* is from Southampton. The Leet Jury drew the attention of the authorities "to Laurence Durvell, who is the son of a former Sheriff." "Seeing the miserable estate to which he has fallen, we desire some care may be taken of him, and that he be shipped with some man where he may be governed, or else kept in some house lest some outrage be committed by him." The following year the jury again asked that something should be done for him, for they "would have him kept in a house, and not allowed to drink so much as he does, for no doubt it would restore him to his wonted mind again." The authorities, however, had no facilities for dealing with such cases, and from a further note it appears that Durvell "was shipped to the Low Countries." (19)

The development and popularity of the town ale-house which so disconcerted the rulers was partly due to the evo-lution of a new working-class in the town seeking social intercourse. Great economic changes were taking place, and the consequent social changes were not understood. Nevertheless, the authorities understood the evil effects of over-drinking, and the regulations adopted to control the trade were so sound that they are still enforced.

NOTES

1. Harrison, *Description of England*, i. Book 2, 158.
2. *Hist. MSS. Comm. Report on the City of Exeter*, 314.
3. Harrison, *Description of England*, 160.
4. Harrod's *Borough of Colchester*, 37.
5. *Coventry Leet Book*, iii. 724.
6. *Gloucester Records, Hist. MSS. Comm. Report* 12, App. Part ix. 435, 472.
7. *Southampton Leet Records*, i. 186.
8. *Manchester Records*, i. 241.
9. *Coventry Leet Book*, iii. 770, 781, 785.
10. 5–6 Ed. VI. Ch. 25.
11. *Norwich Records*, ii. 177.
12. *Manchester Records*, i. 60, 68.
13. *Oxford Records*, 107, 120.
14. *Coventry Leet Book*, iii. 785, 808.
15. Harrison, *Description of England*, i. Book ii. 152.
16. Bacon, *Ipswiche*, 275.
17. Kendal, *Hist. MSS. Comm. Report* 10, App. Part iv. 315.
18. *Manchester Records*, i. 161, 162, 186.
19. *Southampton Records*, i. 331, 343.

CHAPTER X

THE PROVISION OF ARTIFICIAL LIGHT

THE tallow candle was almost the only source of artificial light during the sixteenth century, and even this crude illuminant was not plentiful. The town authorities made great efforts to secure a good supply, and the importance with which they regarded this can be measured by the heavy fines they imposed on persons who disregarded their regulations. At Ipswich, in the middle of the century, candles were sold at a penny farthing a pound. The "bond" required from a Chandler was £20. A butcher who sold tallow contrary to the regulations had to pay £2, and a Chandler £5. If these sums are multiplied by twelve to conform to present values, some idea of the severity of the fines may be gained.

For no other commodity was the "Assize" fixed with more regularity, and in addition many restrictions were imposed to safeguard the supply of tallow. Usually the butchers were forbidden to sell tallow to persons living out of the town, at Gloucester the penalty being loss of citizenship. At Leicester outside traders could buy tallow if they guaranteed to bring back twelve pounds of candles for every stone of tallow taken. An incident at Gloucester shows that control was essential. The "Assize" for tallow and candles had not been fixed, and the butchers took advantage of the omission to force the Chandlers to contract during Lent a year's supply of tallow. As this was a time when few animals were slaughtered, tallow was scarce and dear, and later candles rose in price. The public outcry against the increased price moved the Council to take action, and after an enquiry they appointed a committee to control all future sales of tallow. (1) The Ipswich authorities tried to control the distribution of tallow by ordering each butcher to deliver his tallow to a particular Chandler.

The Chandlers were as closely regulated as the butchers. In addition to price and weight, quality was taken into consideration, for, contrary to the prevalent idea that the rush wick was universal, cotton wick was common, and often stipulated in the regulations. An incident at Chester emphasizes that the difficulties of enforcing the regulations were increased by the limited area over which the authorities operated. The Chandlers were brought before the Mayor "for breaking the Assize, . . . in spite of being bound." Not only had they charged more than statute price, they had also neglected to supply sufficient candles to meet the needs of the citizens. The Chandlers explained to the Mayor that after the "Assize" had been given tallow had risen in price and the people in Chester were now buying candles in the town for threepence a pound and selling them to people outside for threepence-halfpenny. To meet the situation a fresh "Assize" was declared, which fixed the price at threepence-halfpenny.

The price was often so closely regulated that a small adjustment made all the difference between profit or loss. In one instance at Salisbury, after the "Assize" had been declared, the Chandlers told the Mayor that they could only supply candles at the fixed price while their present stock of tallow lasted. After considering their statements, the Mayor allowed an increase of one farthing in the pound of candles, and one-sixth of a penny on a pound of tallow, and this small alteration satisfied the Chandlers. (2)

The general shortage of candles placed the Chandlers in a strong economic position, and unless controlled they exploited this for greater gain. In many towns they were fined for exceeding the "Assize," and at Chester it was necessary to fix a price at which candles could be exchanged for other goods. A regulation at Ipswich shows that there were ways of securing more than the lawful price, for the authorities compelled all Chandlers to provide a bond of £20 that they would "sell candles without the buying of other wares."

From the *Nottingham Records* it can be seen that when left free to trade, the Chandlers could adopt what might be considered modern methods. At one time the four Chandlers in the town were fined "for combining to keep up the price of candles." Not long afterwards they were again in Court charged with acting together "to keep their prices so long as they think good." This time, however, the high price was said to have been imposed as part of a plan to secure a supply of tallow cheap. It was hoped that the excessive price of candles would so reduce consumption that stocks of tallow would accumulate "till they have it at their own price." The "Assize" does not appear to have been enforced very regularly at Nottingham, for the Chandlers paid the fines, and after a short time again adopted the methods for which they had been condemned. That they had little to learn about marketing can be seen from a later charge against them. "They carry candle to other places and sell them cheaper, and only made exactation at home." (3)

The *Southampton Records* supply a picture of the "Common Chandler," an individual who in small villages had been granted the sole right to make and sell candles. The first recorded appearance of the Chandler at the Court was not for ignoring the "Assize," but "because he neither serves poor or others properly—and people want good language and fair speech when they come for candle—because they pay for them." At a later appearance the charge was that though "he had been bound to serve the town at twopence the pound, having the whole of the tallow at a price to his liking, and all others having been restrained, now when there is a scarcity of tallow for one year, . . . he is charging fourpence a pound." Then the writer adds in comment: "A happy man that can make his bargain so well, to take it when there is a profit or refuse to serve when the profit

G

faileth, and to raise it at his own will for his best advantage, to tye all men, and himself be at liberty." For some years this Chandler continued to appear at Court to answer charges of breaking the "Assize," and finally the clerk must have given him up in despair, for in a marginal note he adds, "these are irregular people and it passeth our understanding to deal with them." (4)

As some means of obtaining artificial light was so essential and yet so difficult to secure, it is not surprising to find that towns at last endeavoured to solve the problem in other ways than that of mere regulation. At Leicester the authorities tried to secure supplies by giving the wax Chandlers a monopoly, and passed a by-law that "no man shall work wax neither in taper nor candle to be sold but those that be wax chandlers." For this privilege the craft undertook to supply the town with sufficient tallow candles at one penny a pound, but very soon there was a shortage and the authorities again adopted regulation by the "Assize." At Coventry the Chandlers were well organized, and for a long time had a monopoly, the householders only being allowed to make for their own use. The "Assize" was fixed with great regularity, and by strict regulations, enforced by heavy fines, the town authorities tried to procure a sufficient supply. Then, in 1523, the Council made a change that must have been an innovation and probably caused no little trouble among the crafts. People who were not Chandlers were given the exclusive right to supply the town with candles. The Council Minutes read that

21 April

1523 For-as-much as Jas Hobson and Ric Nicklyn, butchers, with others have taken upon themselves to be bound to the Mayor of the City, to secure and find all the City sufficient candle at the price of 1¼d a pound at thirteen pounds to the dozen for the space of seven years next ensuing. . . . No person or persons of the Craft of Butchers shall bargain to sell to any person of the City, any tallow, only to said Hobson and Nicklyn or others appointed with them.

Of this adventure in private enterprise during the period
of craft domination no particulars are given, except that
seven persons were concerned in the scheme. That it worked
satisfactorily can be assumed from the silence of the *Records*.
For years without a break the "Assize" had been fixed twice
each year, and then for seven years there is not one reference
to the matter. In 1530 the contract ended, and the "Assize"
regulations began again. During the years covered by the
contract the status of those working at the craft must have
changed, for they could only have continued as wage-
earners under the contractors. This is made clear at the
end of the contract period. People desiring to enter the
trade were to be admitted by the Mayor; inspectors were
appointed to enter any place where candles were made and
to test the weight of the candles, and regulations were made
suitable for the oversight of a new body of traders.

The authorities wished to obtain the same smooth working
that had characterized the contract, so, instead of declaring
the "Assize" in the ordinary way, made arrangements for
joint meetings with all those engaged in the trade, at which
the prices of raw materials and finished products were to be
amicably settled, "so that the town be served better cheap
than other towns here about." Unfortunately quarrels arose
almost immediately between the Chandlers and the butchers,
and the Council had to adopt harsh measures to control
both. Later, the Chandlers disputed the right of people outside the town to sell candles in the town market, but as any
increase in the supply was welcomed by the inhabitants,
the Council was compelled to protect the country traders.
For some years the authorities tried to make the scheme a
success, but finding this impossible, reverted to the earlier
method of regulation by the "Assize," and this continued
for many years. (5)

One or two other attempts made by town authorities to
secure adequate supplies are very interesting. In the same
year that the Coventry contract ended, "W. Lobbe" was

elected Mayor of Salisbury, and he decided during his year of office to show how candle-making should be carried on. The two persons—one a woman—who had previously supplied the town were to cease doing so, and the Mayor undertook to provide candles for one penny a pound during the summer and three-halfpence in winter, and to give thirteen pounds to the dozen. In November of the following year he rendered an account of the year's work. The total weight of the tallow brought in was "eight thousand one hundred and sixty nine dozens, ten and twelve pounds" (probably one hundred and fifty-six thousand, two hundred and nineteen pounds). "Five thousand one hundred and sixty-four dozen" were used in the town and the remainder sold in the country districts. Having demonstrated that not only could the City be well supplied, but even the outside districts could be catered for, he resigned the work, and the two former Chandlers were ordered to commence and "keep the town as well supplied as during the past year." Matters were allowed to go on unchecked for six years, then six Chandlers were given the monopoly of the trade, being "bound" to make candle at a fixed price and to pay the butchers "in ready money" for the tallow. Two years later "they were fined twenty shillings for breaking their bond." In 1547 the authorities decided to make and supply candles, but how long they continued the manufacture is not stated. Ten years later Chandlers were again producing, for then one was fined £4 for some contravention of the regulations, and £4 was so heavy a fine that he was allowed over twelve months to complete the payment. (6)

One other instance, that of Ipswich, will serve to show how a municipal authority, after attempting to secure sufficient supplies by a system of rigorous control, was driven to the manufacture of such a common necessary. For the first half of the century production was controlled by the "Assize" as in other towns. In 1536 a regulation stated that a trader would be fined fourpence for every

pound of tallow or candles he sold outside his own town, and
the Council Minutes show this to have been no idle threat,
for in 1539 "divers persons were fined £5 each—being four
pence the pound of candles sold contrary to the former
order, and two certain Chandlers to be bound in £10 each,
not to sell above the rate." At the same meeting the Council
decided to adopt a rationing scheme for distributing tallow,
for the butchers "were to be equally divided among the
Chandlers." In 1541 the authorities found it necessary to
bind the Chandlers in sums of £20 to sell candles without
compelling customers to purchase other goods, obviously
one way by which the "Assize" could be circumvented.
One offender who had incurred a penalty of £20 was only
fined £5 on giving his word not to offend again. In 1548
changes were made. Two men were to be "Common
Chandlers" for seven years, and all other Chandlers were
suspended; butchers were ordered to sell all tallow to the
appointed Chandlers or forfeit their right to trade in the
town. Tallow became almost unobtainable in the following
year, and the scheme broke down. For the next five years
the authorities yearly elected two Chandlers to supply the
town, these being "bound" in a sum of one hundred marks.
Later, to make control easier, each Chandler had to supply
a section of the town; afterwards two others were added, the
four to supply a ward each.

The greatest difficulty lay in securing supplies of tallow.
Probably the price fixed was not economic, for a regulation
which gave the price at which candles could be sold in the
town provided that they might be sold "to strangers at other
market rates." In 1554, for refusing to sell at the "Assize"
price, one butcher was fined 20s., and another disfranchised—
the latter punishment being very severe, for it prevented
him from trading in the town. Almost every year the regulations were made more drastic. A "scavenger" was appointed
to see all cattle killed, and thus check the quantity of tallow
that was produced; and in 1560 the butchers were ordered

to reserve only two pounds of tallow "for victuals" from each beast killed, a fine of 40s. being set for the first offence, half of which was offered to any informant. In the following year the "bond" of the Chandlers was increased to £40, but two years later it was seen that, with the most strict regulation, sufficient candles could not be obtained and a rationing scheme was inaugurated, "the inhabitants to be rated to a certain quantity of candle to be spent by them." The authorities persisted until 1575 to secure supplies by close regulation, and then not having succeeded, the position was reviewed and the problem was passed to a Committee of twelve Councillors.

This Committee decided to centralize production, and as it was already the rule for all butchers to take their tallow to a building set apart for the purpose, the Chandlers were ordered to work in this building. They were determined to enforce all the regulations, and all butchers and Chandlers, or people standing bond for them, were summoned to the Town Court, and told that their bonds, which were very heavy, would be forfeited for any breach; but in spite of this warning some butchers defaulted and their "bonds" were sued. At the end of the year the Committee again reviewed the position, and as a result of the year's experience advised the Council to undertake the production of candles. A loan was floated to secure the "furniture" used in the work, and a rate levied on the inhabitants to supplement the money borrowed. In 1576 the work started under the care of the Committee, and in each succeeding year a Committee of Management was elected. By 1583 the department had become so important that a "treasurie" was needed to keep the accounts, and was prosperous enough to pay his salary "out of the profits." (7)

The many expedients of the authorities to secure a sufficient supply of candles show the difficulties of the problem, but they also prove that the Councils were not afraid to try new methods. Many will be interested in the fact that a municipal supply seems to have been the real solution.

NOTES

1. *Gloucester, Hist. MSS. Comm. Report* 12, App. Part ix. 452.
2. *Salisbury, Hist. MSS. Comm. Report on Various Collections,* iv. 214.
3. *Nottingham Records,* iv. 308, 316, 361.
4. *Southampton Records,* i. 196, 256, 345.
5. *Coventry Leet Book,* iii. 650, 723.
6. *Salisbury, Hist. MSS. Comm. Report on Various Collections,* iv. 215, 216, 219, 221.
7. Bacon's *Ipswiche,* 232, 337.

CHAPTER XI

THE FIRE BRIGADE

DURING the sixteenth century devastating fires were common, for the thatched roofs of the timbered houses were easily ignited and the flames spread rapidly from one house to another. The *Tiverton Records* witness how simply a fearful fire originated and how quickly it spread. Within a small cottage the flames from a blazing frying-pan reached the roof, and although it was market day, with hundreds of people about, the fire could not be subdued, and in a few hours Tiverton had almost disappeared. Four hundred houses were destroyed and over fifty persons are said to have perished.

But many of the worst fires started at maltkins or bakehouses. From a malthouse at Bury St. Edmunds spread a fire which destroyed the greater part of the town, and did damage estimated at £60,000; and at Chester a fire that started in a bakehouse destroyed thirty dwelling-houses and a number of other buildings. The chief danger at bakehouses arose from great stacks of gorse or brushwood stored by the bakers as fuel for their ovens, for once one of these became ignited the flames and sparks were a menace to all surrounding buildings. Because of such fires many town authorities had special by-laws for these premises. At Manchester they prohibited the erection of fuel stacks within thirty feet of any building, (1) and at Chester the proposed site had to be inspected and a permit obtained before any fuel stack could be made. The regulations relating to malthouses aimed at isolating these places so that in case of fire only one building was involved. Leicester and Northampton had by-laws of this kind, but from the *Northampton Records* it can be seen that it was not easy to enforce them. The Council ordered the malsters to close all kilns in the centre of the town and restart on sites approved by the Council. Some refused, and the by-law was only completely enforced after a struggle which lasted for five years, during which the Council appealed both to the Queen and to the Privy Council. (2)

During the century the risk of fire was increased by the extended use of coal. Fireplaces and chimneys became necessary, but so crudely were these made that the authorities were compelled to control their erection. Oxford, Norwich, and Coventry authorities had to forbid the use of wood or turf in making chimneys, and at Kendal property-owners were forbidden to let any building as a dwelling-house unless it had properly constructed fireplaces and chimneys. Practically every town made by-laws to enforce chimney-sweeping at regular intervals, and Norwich had an official Inspector of fireplaces and chimneys. The by-laws also provided that people should be fined if either their house or chimney caught fire. At Exeter the fine for a house fire was 20s. and for a chimney 6s. 8d.; but a man who appeared at Canterbury Court charged with having his chimney ablaze was forgiven his fine "in that he was very poor."

However picturesque thatched roofs may have looked, experience proved that they were dangerous. Even before the beginning of the century Coventry had decided on tiles for roofing, and thatch was completely banished, but in this it appears to have stood almost alone. In 1509 Norwich tried to abolish thatched roofs, but the by-law was strongly opposed and had to be rescinded. Not for many years did they attempt to replace the thatched roofs by a less combustible material. In 1570 a by-law was adopted that no new building should be thatched, "and all repairs that extend to six spars shall be done in tile, lead or slate," "for because of thatched houses, fires have been common and easily spread." (3) Towards the end of the century thatched roofs were generally condemned; nevertheless it must have seemed a drastic measure when in 1582 the Oxford authorities decided that all thatched roofs should be replaced by tiles, lead or slate, and allowed the inhabitants only a short time in which to complete the change. In 1608 Ipswich Council enforced a similar policy, allowing three months for the by-law to be carried out. Bury St. Edmunds, Southampton, and Reading followed this example.

Arrangements for dealing with fires were made by all towns. These usually consisted in providing buckets, ladders of various lengths, and a number of long poles known as croomes. The latter, of wood or iron, had a long hook at one end, and at the other some arrangement for attaching a chain or rope. When it was thought necessary to ensure the safety of the town by demolishing a building near the fire, the hook of the croome was thrust into the roof, and by attaching a horse to the rope or chain, or with the help of a few men, the place could be demolished in a few minutes. A good supply of buckets was usually provided. Chester bought one hundred and Oxford one hundred and ten at one time, while at Northampton and Ipswich every citizen was supposed to provide one. At the latter place the members of the Council made a periodical inspection to see if the by-law was being carried out. Fires were not so common at Coventry, and the authorities were satisfied with an arrangement whereby one bucket was provided by every three citizens. Towards the end of the century the obligation to provide buckets became general, and at Chester and Ipswich persons qualifying for citizenship had to provide a bucket in addition to the ordinary entrance fee. The buckets were made of leather, and four dozen bought in London cost Lincoln nearly £6. Many similar buckets are preserved in country mansions, while a number of village churches still retain the croomes or firehooks.

Though it was usual for the citizens to provide buckets direct, ladders and croomes were always purchased by the Council out of a tax levied for that purpose; and while the buckets remained in the homes of the citizens or were stored in the church, croomes and ladders were kept at convenient places in the streets, and an official appointed to look after them. So strong are local customs that in many towns where these early precautions were in force ladders are still kept under the same condition to-day.

Although every authority believed it to be its duty to provide appliances for fighting fires, there seem to have been few attempts at organizing the work, and citizens were expected to work together until a fire was subdued. At Winchester the inhabitants were ordered "to have standing at their door both day and night in the summer, one tub of water . . . to be cast out in the morning, and filled again." (4) Norwich and Cambridge were exceptions. At these places the authorities in organizing their resources provided the nearest approach to the establishment of a fire brigade. At Norwich the method adopted was the usual one of providing buckets and ladders and storing them in the parish churches; in addition the inhabitants of every ward had at their own cost "to have prepared and hung in some convenient place, one croome of iron with ring and ropes fastened to the same, and four great ladders to serve when needed, the key to be kept by some inhabitant near-by." When a fire occurred "the warning bell was rung," and at its sound "every carrier and every brewer to be ready with horse and cart to get vessels and carry water to the fire" . . . "and to continue during the fire or till dispensed with." These arrangements were continued for a few years, and then, with the completion of the town water supply works, it became possible to improve the organization. Water could be obtained from the taps at various places in the town, and the engineer was "during a fire to supply as much water as is required, or possible." (5) At Cambridge the University and town authorities made a joint agreement. A plentiful supply of buckets, ladders, and croomes was provided, and a small Committee representing both bodies was appointed. On the outbreak of fire two members of the

Committee took charge of the attempts to extinguish the fire, and the other two became responsible for keeping order and for preventing any attempt to steal or remove goods under cover of the confusion caused by the fire. After a fire all buckets and ladders used had to be returned to the various churches, for these were the selected storage places. To complete the organization, churchwardens were required to present an annual report of all fire appliances entrusted to their care. (6)

The *Records* show that after fires the towns helped each other. At Nantwich in 1583 a fire destroyed eight hundred houses, and the *Leicester* and *Nottingham Records* show that a rate was levied in those places for the purpose of helping Nantwich, while officials were collecting in other towns. In 1587 a fire at Beccles caused damage estimated at £20,000, and a rate was levied at Ipswich to aid in the rebuilding. The *Lincoln Records* show that money was granted to other places that had suffered in a similar way. Church Stretton received aid from Shrewsbury, and Exeter assisted Tiverton twice in five years, sending £5 on the first occasion and £100 on the second.

Individuals suffered great loss in isolated outbreaks. The *Shrewsbury Records* mention the case of "John Shelvocke" who had his house, barn, books and all his goods, valued at £60, "destroyed by fire," and ministers were asked "to bring it to the notice of their parishioners that he may receive some relief." The same *Records* give particulars of the plight of "John ap Rees." The Bailiffs had to notify the Brotherhood that this man "who by sudden rage of fire has lost house and all he had" . . . "has been granted a licence to receive charitable gifts."

After an extensive fire some of the property-owners, for various reasons, did not rebuild. In such cases the area became unsightly, even if the partially destroyed buildings were not dangerous. So the authorities were confronted with a situation similar to the slum-clearing problem of to-day.

But at that time the law provided a simple remedy. Such buildings and lands were formally declared derelict, and unless within a prescribed time the owners demolished the buildings and fenced the land became the property of the town. (7)

NOTES

1. *Manchester Records*, ii. 50.
2. *Northampton Records*, ii. 242.
3. *Norwich Records*, ii. 107, 120, 137.
4. Bailey, *Winchester*, 121.
5. *Norwich Records*, ii. 137.
6. Cooper's *Cambridge*, ii. 336.
7. *Norwich Records*, ii. 122, 123.

CHAPTER XII

THE SUPPLY OF FUEL

By the middle of the century fuel was becoming scarce, and some town authorities found it necessary to enact by-laws to reserve the nearby woods from the raids of persons who went gathering fuel. Some indication of the shortage is shown by the fact that legacies for the provision of supplies of wood became frequent. At Ipswich £20 was bequeathed "to be laid out yearly in coal and wood, to be sold to the poor at the same price"; this amount would provide about forty tons of coal.

In 1567 Lincoln Council bought twenty tons of coal at Newcastle, sold it to the poor of Lincoln, and then invited private traders to carry on the business. Probably this was too costly an undertaking for private individuals, and nothing further appears to have been done. In 1571 twelve persons were bound over at the Assize "for riotously cutting down and carrying away trees." At once the fuel supply became an important question at the Council meetings. It was acknowledged that a great shortage existed, said to be due to the actions "of the greedy people, who, having succeeded to the property of the religious houses, have cut down, taken away and consumed, all that timber upon which Lincoln had depended for its supplies." The remedy suggested by the Council was that the Foss Dyke should be cleaned so that timber might be brought from the adjoining counties of York, Derby, and Nottingham, (1) and as this would benefit the surrounding places it was proposed that Parliamentary sanction should be obtained to assess the cost over all the inhabitants within seven miles of Lincoln. At Rye the authorities said that the scarcity of fuel there was due to the activities of iron and glass works, and that the latter were the greatest offenders, for they required no great equipment and could easily move the works as areas became denuded of trees. (2)

The scarcity of wood made it necessary to find a substitute, and the use of coal rapidly increased. Commenting on this development Harrison describes how in his time "a multitude of chimneys arose—and there did arise so many dusty clouds in the air as to hide the light of the sun." (3) Coal was very difficult to obtain, and as it had usually to be brought by sea from Newcastle and "water carriage was limited to the period between May-Day and the Feast of St. Michaels, sufficient for the winter months had to be brought in during the summer-time." (4) The difficulties and cost seem to have been too great for many traders, and it became necessary for town authorities to take over the provision of coal or wood. The Oxford authorities arranged that when any part of the Queen's woods near the town was sold "a portion should be reserved for the town at a reasonable charge." At Chester in 1587 an arrangement was made that is characteristic of the period. The Council granted a loan to an individual enabling him to start business as a coal merchant, reserving to themselves the right to fix the price. Additional interest attaches to this loan in that the money was advanced out of profits made from municipal trade in another commodity.

Although many towns made efforts to supply fuel, Leicester appears to have been the only town authority that provided a continuous supply of coal. Commencing in 1574, the Earl of Huntingdon gave the Council £6 yearly for seven years, that they might provide fuel for the poorer people. Each year the profit arising from the sale was added to the capital, and at one time this amounted to £70, which would purchase nearly one hundred and fifty tons of coal. About this time many schemes to provide employment were set afoot, and the Earl was persuaded that it would be better to spend the money that way, so he asked the Council to use it to establish a clothier in the town. The Council agreed, but they thought that the supply of coal should be continued even if they were compelled to do this on a lesser scale. Only £12 could be secured, so it was felt necessary to restrict the sales to people who were unemployed. The work was carried on by members of the Council, and no difficulty was experienced until the person responsible had the coal delivered at his house instead of at the municipal storage. The offender was ordered to have the whole stock transferred to the proper place, but this incident caused a great deal of trouble and a change in the working of the scheme. The coal fund was increased to £20, and lent to a member of the Council who undertook to provide the coal, and to store and sell it at the old Town Hall. For the use of the Hall and town weights he was to pay £2 yearly, this to be added to the fund. Each year another member took the work. The method of working can best be seen by an extract from the Council Minutes on the matter.

John Clarke had had charge the previous year—and handed over the money at the end of his year. Noted—that the two obligations taken of John Clarke last year—for the providing of coals for the poor and for the repayment of the stock of Money back again were now delivered to the Mayor and by him to the Chamberlains who were upon appointment, to receive the stock of money for the coal from the said John Clarke, which is now £20. And for the use of the coal-house and scales and weights due for the year past from the said John Clarke they are to receive 40/-. Also they are to receive of Mr. William Cotton for the use of coals for the poor, which was given to the town by Mr. Thomas Cotton deceased, the sum of £5. So the whole sum for the stock for coal is now £27. The said Chamberlains now appointed to provide coal, viz.—good coal—Overton coal— for the poor and to serve the poor of this town the year following, after sixpence the hundred; the half hundred, and quarter hundred, at the same rate—to serve at the old Town Hall, Wednesdays and Saturdays, and oftener if required; and the said Chamberlain must pay for the use of the coal-house and weights upon the fourth day of May next coming, 40/- over and above the said £27. So the whole sum they have to pay is £29, and to be bound for the true performance as John Clarke was bound, . . . to bestow the whole stock in coals and carriage, but to buy no coal in the town nor by the way coming into the town.

It is noteworthy that over a period of twenty-five years, during which prices were rising rapidly, the selling price of one hundred pounds of this coal only rose one penny. (5)

During the period two authorities made attempts to find coal in their districts. At Nottingham it was agreed to pay "Robert Handcocke and his two workmen . . . ten pence a day to dig in the coppice for search of coals, and to be provided with iron work, two mattocks, one shovel and a herring barrel. To begin at furthest at our Lady Day." (6) Shrewsbury was more ambitious, for the Council decided "that if there shall not amount to the sum of £100 of benevolence towards the finding of the coal-pit there shall be an assessment of those not benevolent towards the same." The adventure must have succeeded, for the report adds that there "were found great stores of coal . . . the which is like to be of great commodity both for rich and poor." William Gardner, Dyer, appears to have carried out the work and "he is worthy to be had in remembrance for ever." (7)

As coal came into common use town authorities made regulations as to its sale, and those of the Gloucester Council serve to show how thorough these were. The selling price was fixed and the sacks were to be made to hold the correct measure. If the buyer wished, the contents had to be measured at the time of sale, and if faulty the coal was to be seized and the sacks burnt. (8)

NOTES

1. *Lincoln, Hist. MSS. Comm. Report* 14, App. Part viii. 61, 63, 64, 65.
2. *Rye, Hist. MSS. Comm. Report* 13, App. Part iv. 76.
3. Harrison's *Description of England*, i. 239, ii. 178.
4. Welford, *Newcastle and Gateshead*, iii. 63.
5. *Leicester Records*, iii. 160, 414, and iv. 2.
6. *Nottingham Records*, iv. 239.
7. Owen and Blakeway, *Shrewsbury*, i. 347.
8. *Gloucester, Hist. MSS. Comm. Report* 12, App. Part ix. 433.

CHAPTER XIII

THE TOWN AND THE POOR

THE attitude of the town authorities to the problem of poverty is easily understood. Each town was a unit separated almost more completely from the rest than whole countries are to-day. Persons from other towns were not merely strangers, but foreigners. If traders, they were regarded as individuals who, if permitted, would share the profitable trade of the town without contributing to its upkeep; if they were poor, there was the possibility that, sooner or later, they might become a burden on the town. So town authorities tried to exclude both types, and almost any measure that succeeded in doing this was considered justifiable.

In dealing with the poor at the beginning of the century the authorities had little sympathy for the able-bodied persons who would not work. "Big Beggars," as they were called at Coventry, "that will not work to get their living— let them be banished from the town, or else punish them so without favour that they shall be weary to dwell here."

In this Coventry expressed the general attitude of the towns toward the able-bodied unemployed. There were, however, the poor who by reason of age or infirmity could not work, and if natives of the town these were cared for. "It doth belong to the duty of the magistrates to have care of the fatherless, the widow, and the oppressed," wrote the Shrewsbury Bailiffs when making provision for the maintenance and apprenticeship of a neglected orphan boy. But if, without some organization, a town authority gave aid or allowed the poor to beg, they found this allured undesirable people into the town, and in 1500 Gloucester tried to avoid this by enrolling the names "of the native poor that be not mighty in body," and making arrangements for their maintenance. Then, fearing the burden might become too heavy, the authorities decided that once the list was drawn up no more people should be included until one died, when another could "be added in his place and keep their numbers even." Nearly forty years later Chester adopted a similar plan. There, after the list was made, the poor were allotted different wards for begging, and the inhabitants of the wards were supplied with the names of the people to whom they might give alms.

But in practice registration had its limits. Something was required whereby the authorized beggar could be instantly recognized, and Gloucester provided this when in 1504 its thirty-six registered beggars were supplied with "a badge of the aforesaid town." At Leicester badges for the poor are mentioned in 1517, and three years later Shrewsbury authorities "paid eighteenpence for a yard of hempen cloth and for painting seventy-two 'Leopards Heads' to make badges for their accredited beggars when asking for alms." (1)

As a means of quickly recognizing those allowed to solicit alms the badge was a great advance on registration, and was destined sixty years later to be put on a national basis. From painted cloth it was changed to metal, and usually bore the arms of the town or some significant words such as "The City of Norwich, Impotent Person." Coventry adopted the system in 1521, and everyone "admitted to beg was to have a token on their badge the sign of the Olyphant and they that have not the token not to be allowed to dwell in the City." Lincoln, Canterbury, and King's Lynn adopted an official token before its use was ordered by the Poor Law Statute of 1562. Although the badge was introduced by Gloucester in 1504, it was not adopted at Ipswich until 1557, and by Northampton until 1585. Newcastle must have had an inordinate number of poor, for the local authorities issued one hundred and thirty-seven badges at one time, as against fifty at Norwich, seventy-two at Shrewsbury, and forty at Oxford.

The numbers of beggars increased as the century advanced, and after the middle of the century, when relief was becoming more general in the towns, the authorities realized the importance of a clause that first appeared in the Poor Law Statutes of 1530–31, and was re-enacted in subsequent legislation. This provided that any person who could prove continuous residence in one parish for three years gained the right to remain and be relieved, and it is certain that no other clause in the Poor Law Statutes of the century so dominated and decided the actions of the authorities as did this one. Mere negligence might cause the town to be saddled with an intolerable burden; for, although the badge made it possible to distinguish between native and alien poor, it did not prevent the latter from staying in the town, and the authorities had to devise methods to keep them from securing a settlement there.

The Statute of 1495 had given the authorities power to punish and expel undesirable beggars, and in most towns this duty was assigned to the Aldermen, who at Coventry were "to make due search for vagabonds and lusty beggars, and cause them to avoid out of their ward—under pain of imprisonment . . . women as well as men." Later it became usual to appoint officials, known as "Beadles of the Poor." At Lincoln this official was "to have 20/- yearly for ordering of the poor and driving away and punishing vagabonds, strange beggars, and poor people." At Manchester for many years the Beadle was elected annually with the rest of the town officials, and at one time was allowed fourpence extra for every beggar he had whipped. Toward the end of the century his services were dispensed with, but the authorities soon realized that it was "useful and profitable to have a Beadle . . . it keeps beggars from coming, and prevents those from begging who are being relieved."

The Beadle was probably a sinister figure in the lives of those unhappy people who were unable to find a permanent home, and it is some consolation to know that, however necessary he may have been, he was controlled. The *Norwich Records* relate that, "upon complaint made by two men and two women against Purdey Hurde, and understood, . . . It is ordered by the Court that his staff belonging to the Master of the Beggars shall be taken off him, and he is to be discharged from the said office and committed to the stocks." (2)

Undesirable as sturdy beggars might be, the town authorities saw the possibility of a yet greater danger. During periods of prosperity workers were drawn into the towns, and the authorities feared that the families of these people might eventually become a burden on the rates. How far this fear led them to develop a policy of exclusion is shown by the action of the Chester authorities, who declared that "Whereas daily inconvenience and great charge has arisen . . . in that certain persons for their own private profit have built within the city, . . . cottages, and have placed labourers therein who in a few years' time have wives and children maintained only by their daily labour, who when it pleased God to visit them or they have died, . . . their wives and children become common beggars; and to avoid the same it is now ordered that no citizen or other inhabitant shall build or cause to be built, any such cottages in this City." (3)

This policy was generally adopted. At Nottingham, where was a great shortage of houses, cottages were built and barns converted into houses, yet the builder, an Alderman, was "presented" at the Town Court and ordered to desist. (4) Another regulation intended to achieve the same result forbade any person to let a house or rooms to any stranger who had not been interviewed by the Mayor. If the property-owner infringed this regulation, a heavy fine was imposed. (5)

Great hardship ensued when this regulation was only enforced at intervals, as people who had settled in a town found shortly before the end of their three years' residence that the authorities had put the order into force, and if their position was not considered satisfactory by some official, they were obliged to leave the town. This happened at Oxford in 1582 and at Leicester in 1576. At the latter place it was realized that the order was against the interests of some property-owners, and "two honest men without property were elected to see the order obeyed."

Town *Records* give little idea of the hardship that this policy must have inflicted upon the unfortunate people who were not natives of the town. Victims of circumstances beyond their control, their lot was made harder by the very statute intended to protect them. Few greater blunders could have been made than to give them the right to "poor relief" by a statute that did not provide the necessary finance nor the administrative machinery to make it workable. It certainly was a great factor in preventing natural settlement by absorption. Driven from proper dwelling-houses, the people crowded into barns or similar buildings, which were converted into rude cottages, and even then, if these places were within the limits of the town, because of the Act, they were still persecuted and driven away. (6)

There is plenty of evidence that within the town, not only were the lesser-known clauses of the Poor Law being carried out, but the authorities were assisting the poor in many ways. At Ipswich a children's hospital or training-school was established at a cost of £86, (7) and at Bury St. Edmunds some of the poor were provided with spinning-wheels. (8) At Lincoln an allowance of three shillings and fourpence was made to a woman for bringing up an illegitimate child whose parents were dead, (9) and at Nottingham the father of another illegitimate child was traced and compelled to pay toward its maintenance until the child was fourteen. (10) When an old man applied for relief at Chester, his wealthy son was compelled to pay him a regular allowance. (11) Boarding-out of paupers was known, and for one man at Nottingham an innkeeper agreed to "provide on his own free will, as much meat, bread, and drink

as was necessary, and to receive from the parish, four-pence
weekly." (12)

The Chamberlain rolls show how diverse were the calls
for aid to which the towns responded. Those of Nottingham
for 1579, among other things, record the following gifts:—

To a poor blind man	4d
Paid for a pair of shoes for the neatherd's boy	12d
Given to a poor woman being borne to Lenton	6d
Given to a poor man dwelling in Southwell his house being burnt	6d
Given to two lame soldiers	6d
To a poor man that had his house burned	6d
To a cripple conveyed from town to town	6d
To four lame men from Kendal going to the baths	12d

Other town *Records* reveal how widespread was this kind of
relief. At Beverley lame children were placed in the care of
selected women, who were recompensed by the authority. (13)
At Canterbury "blind Joan Clyton" received an annuity
for at least twenty years. (14) At Norwich an official was
ordered to pay 2s. weekly "to a poor woman that lyeth in
childbed" . . . "until he hath charge to the contrary"; (15)
and at Leicester 1s. 4d. was given "to a poor girl for a pair
of shoes." An interesting fact is that the "Parish" or "Town
Doctor" existed long before the nineteenth century. In the
sixteenth century, town authorities provided a free doctor
for the poor, and also paid for the services of a specialist,
when such were necessary. Those who received parish relief
at Ipswich were to have "surgery and physic at the town's
charge." (16) At Newcastle, "John Coulson, Surgeon," was
paid "his accustomed fee for helping to cure the poor,
maimed people, and Robert Smith, Physician, received a
yearly salary of £20." (17) The Chester town doctor was to
"undertake to the best of his power, to see, cure and heal all
the diseased, sick, poor people that live by alms." (18) At
Canterbury Thomas Pullen received "his fee for being a
Surgeon ready to help such in the city as have not the means

to pay for his help." (19) At Shrewsbury "Doctor Wysbeche and his Lady, both practitioners in physic," who had served the town poor free for twenty years, were provided with a pension by a public subscription. (20) Where doctors were not specially appointed other arrangements were made to provide the poor with medical aid. At Canterbury "two surgeons and their fellows" were paid "for cutting off the leg of lame Joan Steling," (21) and at Norwich an official was ordered "to buy, every Saturday and Wednesday, a rack of mutton or veal for the poor lame boy, which is put to William Fever, Surgeon, to be cured." (22) At Norwich a man "very skilful in bone-setting" received £4 a year and a free house "to attend without charge such as shall have the misfortune to have their legs, arms, or other bones broken, and be poor and not able to pay for their healing." (23) It was common to send people to the various towns where mineral springs were reputed to cure certain ailments, and "the poor lame boy" in the almshouse at Oxford "was to have 6/8 or 10/– to go to the new well for his cure." (24) This may have been the new well at Bath, recently opened for the use of the poor, for whose convenience the town authorities had "supplied three tons of timber and four hundred laths to build a house adjoining." (25)

The help given to the poor was not confined to methods suggested by statutes or regulations. The failure of the harvest in 1597 caused a famine in many parts of the country, and at Bristol "it was concluded upon by Master Mayor and the Council that every Alderman with the rest of the worshipful, and every burger that was of any worth, should every day give one meal a day to so many people that wanted work, some eight, some six, some four, some two, according to their ability . . . whereby the poor of our City were all relieved and kept from starving." (26)

At Ipswich one member of the Council suggested that poor relief should be paid on Sunday afternoons at the church and restricted to those who had attended the service.

THE GRAMMAR SCHOOL

His proposal was not adopted, and the *Records* are singularly free from charges which reflect against either the officials who administered the funds or those who received them. Two examples will suffice to illustrate some of the minor offences. At Nottingham an official appears to have taken advantage of a person who had little idea of the value of money, for the Chamberlain's accounts contain an item "given to a poor woman that keeps a child that was found in the town and was to have had quarterly 16d., and in consideration of 2/6 in hand hath discharged the town thereof." (27) At Shrewsbury the Bailiff was informed that "Richard Sandbrookes' wife had applied for fourpence more weekly, and as the man has fourpence weekly from Mrs. P., and has of his own one cow, one heifer, seven sheep, besides geese, hens and a good store of household goods," the writer wished to know if it should be granted. (28)

The Poor Law Statute of 1572 authorized local authorities to levy a rate on the parish for the maintenance of the poor, but this was merely extending town practice. Long before this town authorities had levied poor rates and enforced their payment, and the Norwich *Records* show how rates assessed on the citizens took the place of the freewill offering. In 1548 an Alderman "certified to the court" that when Andrew Quasshe was asked by the gatherer for the twopence due from him, he replied, "I will give you but one penny—and contemptuously shook his head saying, so tell your Aldermen." This defiance roused the Council, for each Alderman was instructed to prepare a list of the names of every person in his ward, the amount of money that was gathered toward the poor, and the sum each parishioner paid. When this information had been secured, a Committee was formed in each ward to assess the amount every citizen should pay to the maintenance of the poor. Failure to pay was met by imprisonment. (29) At Coventry in 1547 the poor were relieved from the ordinary town funds, and at Cambridge in 1556 the inhabitants were taxed for poor relief. Nor did the parish become at once the unit of organization, for the towns continued their old methods of raising money. At Chester, many years after the passing of the Act, the poor rate was still levied on the ward, and at Liverpool in 1592, and at Northampton in 1585, begging was still organized. At the last town twenty-one persons had badges, and "seven were to go for two days to the inns, and the next two days seven again . . . and so on till they completely beg the town."

The *Cambridge* and *Leicester Records* show how varied were the sources upon which the authorities could draw. At Cambridge every person requiring the seal of the town on a document had to give one shilling to the poor-box in addition to the ordinary fee, as had those who were admitted into citizenship. Persons who lost their case in the Town Courts were compelled to contribute, and "every attorney, their fees having almost doubled," had to pay one penny out of every fee received. (30) Leicester had a scheme to raise an auxiliary fund for the poor that must have been unique, for it was based on the marriage and birth rates. A custom had grown of holding expensive feasts after the "churching" of a woman, and in 1536 the Mayor of Chester protested against the practice on the grounds that people went to far greater expense than they could rightly afford. In 1568 Leicester decided that some of the money that otherwise would have been spent on these occasions should be used to assist the poor. Feasts at "churchings" were forbidden—"save only one dish of meat for gossips and midwives"—and a scale of payments was fixed which applied to both weddings and churchings. At his marriage, or at the churchings of his wife, an Alderman had to pay 2s. 8d., a Councillor 1s. 4d., and a Commoner 4d., and an official was appointed to attend the churches and collect the money. Sometimes gifts had to be discounted. On passing through Leicester the Earl of Huntingdon left twenty "nobles" to be given to the poor, and this was so

well distributed that it averaged three-halfpence each. But
the Chamberlain's accounts show that the Earl was given
a hogshead of wine costing £4 10s., "two fat oxen that
cost twenty marks," and supper, bed and breakfast at
£2 18s. 8d. Later he added to his gift by a present of six
bucks to the Council.

But the towns did not depend solely upon the money
received from taxes and collections. Money and property
were often bequeathed for the use of the poor, and taking
into consideration the difference in value of money and the
smaller population of the towns then as compared with
now, it will be seen that the value of these gifts was considerable. A sum of £100 was received by Norwich, and one
of £133 and another of £50 by Exeter. Tiverton received
£200 under the will of one individual. Ipswich and Lincoln
received £60 and £40 respectively. There were numerous
smaller legacies and gifts. At Salisbury, Thomas Bricket
ordered that "the five almshouses that I have builded in
Dragon St. be given to the use of five poor men or women
. . . and I will that the Mayor and his Brethren take the
rent of two houses adjoining . . . to see the said almshouses well repaired." (31) This method of providing for
the aged poor was one of the pleasing features of the time,
and became more frequent as the century advanced.

Many of the authorities provided facilities for a free
education. At Nottingham early in the century, "because by
learning the public weal commonly is governed," Dame
Agnes Meller "bequeathed land and buildings to begin,
erect, found, create, establish, and make one free school for
one Master and one Usher to teach Grammar everlasting,
to be called the Free School of Nottingham." After the death
of the first Trustees the town authorities were to take over
the control, and in 1516 a portion of the town common was
enclosed, and the rent devoted to the upkeep of the
School. (32) The Shrewsbury School was started in 1548,
and in 1564 an assessment for its maintenance was made in

all the parishes. A few years later the town Bailiffs were enquiring as to their right to found University Scholarships. (33) In 1551 Thomas Chipsey, a grocer of Northampton, bequeathed lands to "provide a master to teach Grammar free of charge to those boys who desired it." Six years later the town authorities approached Cardinal Pole and secured the disused Church of St. Gregory "for the building of a schoolhouse and a house for a Master." At Leicester also an old church was the first building to be used as a Town School, "St. Peter's" being adapted for that purpose in 1563. Ten years later the Council bought the church of the Queen "and covenant and grant to our Lady . . . to build and set up in the space of one year after the date here, a substantial school house fit for children to be taught in . . . with windows and door and covered with tiles." The school was completed the following year. The Chamberlain's books show that the Queen and the Earl of Huntingdon contributed towards the maintenance of a "Free School"; that a rate was levied on the townspeople, and that the schoolmaster received a salary of £12 16s. 8d. One other item is interesting: 1s. 4d. is received "of the boys of the said school toward the mending of a window broken at the shutting of the Master forth of the School." Nearly two centuries later, "Barring Out" or excluding the masters from the school on the eve of the holidays was an established custom, and it may be that it was practised as early as the sixteenth century.

Liverpool commenced its Free School in 1556, with a gift from the Queen and an assessment on the town. At Manchester the School was maintained from the profits from the manorial corn-mill, and the authorities complained that "many not regarding the commonweal and good education of their children in ye school, wilfully absent themselves and grind at other mills." They point out that this will lead to the overthrow of the School and ask for fuller support, and "if the Miller is at fault two persons will be put in to amend the same." The authorities, not certain that kind words would suffice, added "and if this our gentle request will not serve, think it no uncourtesy if we use such means as we may lawfully do." (34) At Lincoln, from the beginning of the century, there are many references to a Grammar School. The first School probably belonged to the Church, but at one time the town authorities were paying the school-master's salary. In 1568 Robert Mounson was "pleased to make a Free School at his own charge in the late Grey-friars," and in 1584 the two Schools were united. In 1588 the town authorities decided to pension the schoolmaster "because he is old, and doth no good upon the children." (35) Many authorities provided scholarships to the Universities, and sons of poor men found it possible to stay and take their M.A. degree. From Bridgnorth it can be seen that early in the century the conflict between secular and Church authorities was beginning. The Council decided "that no priest shall keep any school save only one child to help him say mass after a school master comes to town, but that every child resort to the common school." (36)

The working out by the town authority of schemes of poor relief is of great interest, for their experiments were the basis of national legislation. Although determined not to suffer strangers, they never tried to evade their responsibility to the native poor. Unlike nineteenth-century legislators, they did not confuse "the poor in deed" with the "sturdy vagabond," and it was for the control of the latter that the House of Correction was built. Free education, free medical aid for the poor, relief for the needy, and homes for the aged was the policy of the town rulers. Even if their aims were not fully realized, their effort commands respect.

NOTES

1. *Shrewsbury, Hist. MSS. Comm. Report* 15, App. Part x. 32.
2. *Norwich Records*, ii. 174.
3. *Chester, Hist. MSS. Comm. Report* 8, Part i. 452.
4. *Nottingham Records*, iv. 192, 237, 238.
5. *Oxford Records*, 422; also *Manchester Records*, i. 248.
6. *Lincoln, Hist. MSS. Comm. Report* 14, App. Part viii. 72; also *Manchester Records*, ii. 288.
7. Bacon's *Ipswiche*, 388.
8. *Bury St. Edmunds, Hist. MSS. Comm. Report* 14, App. Part viii. 140.
9. *Lincoln, Hist. MSS. Comm. Report* 14, App. Part viii. 69.
10. *Nottingham Records*, iv. 230.
11. *Chester*, Early English Text Soc., 173.
12. *Nottingham Records*, iv. 187.
13. *Hist. MSS. Comm. Report on Beverley*, 182.
14. *Canterbury, Hist. MSS. Comm. Report* 9, App. Part i. 158.
15. *Norwich Records*, ii. 191.
16. Bacon's *Ipswiche*, 392.
17. Welford, *Newcastle and Gateshead*, iii. 75, 132.
18. Morris, *Chester*, 357.
19. *Canterbury, Hist. MSS. Comm. Report* 9, App. Part i. 157.
20. *Shrewsbury, Hist. MSS. Comm. Report* 15, App. 157. Part x. 17.
21. *Canterbury, Hist. MSS. Comm. Report* 9, App. Part i. 158.
22. *Norwich Records*, ii. 190.
23. *Ibid.*, ii. 144.
24. *Oxford Records*, 404.
25. King and Watts, *Records of Bath*, 58.
26. Seyer's *Bristol*, ii. 255.
27. *Nottingham Records*, iv. 231.
28. *Shrewsbury, Hist. MSS. Comm. Report* 15, App. Part x. 53.
29. *Norwich Records*, ii. 174.
30. Cooper's *Cambridge*, ii. 163.
31. *Salisbury, Hist. MSS. Comm. Report on Various Collections*, iv. 217.
32. *Nottingham Records*, iii. 453, 457.
33. *Shrewsbury, Hist. MSS. Comm. Report* 15, App. Part x. 37, 44.
34. *Manchester Records*, i. 186.
35. *Lincoln, Hist. MSS. Comm. Report* 14, App. Part viii. 26, 56, 62, 73.
36. *Bridgnorth, Hist. MSS. Comm. Report* 10, 425.

CHAPTER XIV

UNEMPLOYMENT

HOWEVER much the authorities tried to provide for the poor and needy, they did not forget that employment was the best kind of relief to offer those who could work, and many attempts were made to stimulate the industries of the town, or even to introduce new ones. The efforts of the Coventry authorities show how thoroughly the problem was attacked. The town depended upon its cloth trade, and in 1518 the Council decided to reorganize the industry so that abuses and difficulties would be abolished and employment provided for all. Spinning and weaving were the two most important sections. It was the practice for "Clothiers" to distribute wool to spinners, who spun it into weft in their own homes, and one great complaint of the Clothiers was that the spinners often failed to return the same weight of material as had been supplied. The authorities determined to stop any pilfering, but to ensure justice decided that first the weights used by those who distributed wool must be tested and stamped by an official of the Council. Then all complaints against spinners, either of returning short weight or of faulty work- manship, were to be investigated, and if substantiated the spinners were to be publicly punished. Turning to the employers, the Council insisted that in every case the wages of the workers should be paid in money, "and if they will have cloth or other chaffer, let them, when they have their money, buy it and pay for it."

Regulations were also made to control weaving and finishing cloth. A price-list was made out, which specified the rate to be paid for weaving certain kinds of cloth, and a central building obtained where finished cloth had to be taken and there examined by a Joint Committee of Weavers, Finishers, and Drapers, thus giving all interests some representation. The cloth had to be "viewed over a perch," and this is still the method of examining cloth in modern factories. "And if it be good cloth, as it ought to be in length and breadth that the City may have praise of it and no slander, then set upon it the Oliphant in lead, and on the back of the seal the length of the cloth so that men shall perceive that it is good Coventry cloth."

Stating the length of the cloth on the seal was to prevent merchants from stretching the finished cloth, and thus gain a little in length at the expense of quality. The "Searchers" were instructed to be impartial in their work, and "if any man hath brought any cloth . . . whatever degree he be . . . if it be not able for the good name of the City to let pass . . . let him do his best with it . . . but set not the seal of the City upon it." In this manner the authorities hoped to produce a good quality cloth that would find a ready market.

After making the regulations the Council revealed that an individual had come forward offering to provide "two hundred stones of wool as it cost, the cost paid, and four hundred shillings with it." This had to be delivered "to ten men, twenty stones of wool and forty shillings each, to pay for the spinning and weaving." The money had to be repaid in three instalments spread over the year, after which more wool could be supplied. If the men in charge could not sell all the cloth, arrangements were to be made to buy it from them.

In these regulations there are two very interesting provisions, the insistence on money wages and the establishment of the Joint Committee. During the nineteenth century the central government found it necessary to compel employers to pay wages in money and not in kind or "Chaffer," as the old-time authorities called it, and in the twentieth century the Joint Committee has been re-established.

For many years there was no trouble, but by 1530 the dyers had combined and charged such high prices for dyeing cloth, that in 1532, another dyeing process was adopted. The new dye had been introduced by a Frenchman, but must have been inferior, for the town authorities became greatly alarmed "lest the good name of Coventry cloth should suffer," and ordered the "Searchers" to remove the town seal from all cloth dyed with the new dye. The Council then turned its attention to the Dyers' Gild and by various regulations completely broke down the monopoly.

From later developments it can be inferred that the scheme was a success. In 1549 the Council thought it necessary to assist the trade, and announced that if any Clothier could not sell all his cloth, he was to take it to the Town Hall and they would buy it. (1) Nineteen years later the authorities claimed that they had established the manufacture of two kinds of cloth that had "been chiefly made in Armentières in Flanders," and safeguarded their interests by securing Letters Patent from the Queen, which granted them the sole manufacturing rights in England. (2)

The above efforts had been directed towards the establishment of a particular industry, but in 1547 the authorities decided to examine the more general problem of unemployment. A census was taken in which the inhabitants had to give their name and age, state whether married or single, and give the number of their dependent children. They also had to state whether they were owners or tenants of their dwelling-houses, and if they worked for others or were their own masters. Having thus secured the facts, the Council announced that provision would be made for all who "by reason of infirmity, age, or number of children were not able to support themselves." Regulations were made for those at work, no employer being allowed to discharge a man without a week's notice, and no man could leave his master until the work in hand was finished. A special Council meeting was held once a month to deal with unemployment, each Alderman having to report on the conditions existing in his own ward. The Council took the responsibility of providing employment for all, and those refusing work were compelled to leave the City at once. (3)

Coventry was not alone in its efforts to provide employment, for most authorities tried in some way to bring trade into their own town. A frequent method was that adopted by Lincoln in 1517; the Council offering to find the capital if a Clothier would commence business in the town. In the following year the freedom of the city was offered to any spinner or cloth-worker who would do this.

After the middle of the century, employment schemes took a new aspect, being no longer destined to stimulate the trade of the town, and the idea emerged of having a central building in which the unemployed could be compelled to work under supervision. This is illuminating, for it reflects the changing industrial structure and the disappearance of the craftsmen working at home. The economic changes that would introduce the industrial revolution were even then beginning. At Lincoln in 1551 there was an attempt to establish a cloth factory, the City offering to find the building and to allow the seal of the City to be affixed to the cloth made. The object was to provide work for the unemployed, but the scheme appears to have been opposed by the Weavers' Gild, and after a short time failed. In 1556 Ipswich elected a Committee to solve the problem of finding work for the unemployed of that town, and a private individual gave a sum toward securing a building where they might be compelled to work. A house was acquired and used for the training of children in some craft, but nothing was done for adults. Norwich in the following year elected a Committee for a similar purpose, but here again nothing came of it. Then in 1564 Salisbury had to consider the problem, and there it was decided to allow no one to beg, but to obtain and equip a building in which people could be compelled to work for their maintenance. Twelve of the Councillors were to control the place, and in this manner the Elizabethan "house of correction" had its beginning. (4)

In 1571 Leicester, Chester, and Norwich were all trying to solve the problem of unemployment. At Leicester it was decided to establish cloth-making, and a "Clothier" was loaned £40 to start the work; later this was increased to £100, the Council having to sell town property to raise part of the money.

At Chester a Committee was formed to devise something "to rid the City of all idle vagrants," and it recommended that "those paying toward the poor should pay four years' money at once, to found and equip a convenient place whereby the poor might apply for work and be relieved." The plan was accepted; the levy brought in about £150, but the building was not opened until 1575 or 1576. Control was vested in a Committee of five, which was "to make yearly accounts, take a reasonable profit, and the rest to go to the poor." (5)

In all the experiments there is the idea of providing special workshops in which able-bodied unemployed might earn their own living, so the successful working out of this idea on a big scale at Norwich must have greatly influenced future schemes. The authorities there said that over two thousand beggars going from door to door cost the City at least £2,000 a year. The inhabitants were chiefly to blame, "for they gave so generously that the poor were attracted, and even some of the workers found it more profitable to cease working and depend on charity." After a census had been taken and the number and condition of the poor ascertained, it was decided to forbid begging and private almsgiving, and to establish houses where both men and women could be compelled to work for their relief.

A "House of Correction" for men was built, and all rogues sent there were to remain twenty-one days and to earn their living. Separate establishments were provided for women and children. For the young children a school was established where they could be taught until they were old enough for service.

To ensure efficient administration the Mayor and four Aldermen were to have control as Commissioners, and take charge of all money collected or bequeathed for the poor. The authorities claimed that the scheme was a great success, and that 950 children, 180 women, and 64 men "that did beg and live idly" were now at work, and that the earnings of these people, added to the amount saved by the removal of beggars from the town, total over £3,000. (6)

Four years after the initiation of the scheme, the Statute of 1575 ordered that a "House of Correction should be established in every County," and every town was to make provision for employing the poor. The Almshouses at Oxford and the "Hospital at Reading" were made into "Houses of Correction," and Ipswich, Cambridge, and Liverpool established places before the end of the century.

The relative unimportance of national social legislation in the sixteenth century as against the important creative work of the town authorities can be well illustrated from the establishment of Houses of Correction. Thirty-three years after Norwich had worked out its scheme, and twenty-nine years after the passing of the Act, a Justice of the Peace of the County of Leicester informed the Mayor of Leicester "that there is an intention in myself and the rest of the Justices to erect a House of Correction according to law," and suggested that a building might be secured in the City. Northampton provides another instance. In 1598 the authorities made an assessment to obtain funds to provide work for the poor. Most of the money collected was spent in giving relief, and it was not until 1615, forty years after the Act was passed, that a House of Correction was established.

There was a great deal of labour regulation in connection with the poor law. By the Statute of 1562 no worker could legally travel without first securing a permit from a magistrate. Few of these are mentioned in town *Records*, but one from Chester is given here. (7)

19 Eliz.
June. To all Mayors, Sheriffs and Bailiffs. Robert Chaffee, Mayor of the City of Exeter, Greeting, for as much as the bearer, George Stampford of this City and Ede his wife being without work are desirous to travel to some convenient place where they may have work for their better relief, and also have with them one child. These are therefore to pray you to suffer the bearers hereof to seek for work without molestation or trouble.

How necessary it was to have a permit is seen by the arrest of four men at the Lincoln Fair. On examination they said they were from London; one had come to see his grand-mother, the second to sell ale, the third to seek work, and the fourth to sell pins and laces. Though the Jury declared that "we can see no fault with the first," orders were given for all four to be placed in the stocks.

All towns endeavoured to bring together those who wanted work and those who needed workmen. At Coventry a regulation required all "carpenters, masons, tilers, daubers, and all kinds of labourers lacking work to be at the Broad-gate with their tools in their hands at five oclock in the summer as in times past they have been, to the intent that they who lack workmen may find them." (8) Almost every town had a similar by-law, and usually the men had to assemble at the Market Cross and remain one hour. That the authorities were vigilant can be seen from the *Norfolk Records*. A man was summoned before the Court, and when asked by what trade he maintained his family, "he could not recite one lawful trade or occupation, whereby he had during the last month, earned anything towards their maintenance."

One other reference will suffice to show how far some authorities went in their attempts to regulate labour. The constables at Bury St. Edmunds were ordered to ask any persons suspected of loitering where they had worked each day of the previous week and at once to verify the answers; further, any labourer who had no work for the coming week was to report, so that work could be provided. (9)

Regulation was the accepted practice, but town *Records* show that the authorities did more than regulate, and their attempts to revive decaying industries or to introduce new ones prove that they did not regard relief as being a substitute for work. The attempt to establish central workshops or factories is one of the best indications of the changes that were taking place in industry.

NOTES

1. *Coventry Leet Book*, iii. 656, 668, 697, 791.
2. *Coventry, Hist. MSS. Comm. Report* 15. App. Part x. 125, 151.
3. *Coventry Leet Book*, iii. 783.
4. *Salisbury, Hist. MSS. Comm. Report on Various Collections*, xiv. 224.
5. Morris, *Chester*, 362, 364.
6. *Norwich Records*, ii. 344, 356.
7. Morris, *Chester*, 358.
8. *Coventry Leet Book*, iii. 807.
9. *Bury St. Edmunds, Hist. MSS. Comm. Report* 14, Part viii. 193.

CHAPTER XV

THE PLAGUE AND OTHER DISEASES

DURING the sixteenth century a number of infectious diseases grouped under the common name of the "Plague," or "The Visitation," brought death and desolation to the towns, and because these diseases have never been fully understood, the period has received an unenviable reputation for bad sanitary conditions. It is therefore necessary to examine the nature and extent of these outbreaks before giving an account of the measures adopted by the different town authorities to prevent or deal with the spread of infection.

The town *Records* bear witness to the number of outbreaks that occur, but there is great difference between the various towns. Cambridge during the first half of the century was seldom free, there being twelve occasions on which it was thought desirable to curtail the University terms. Most of these outbreaks do not appear to have been very serious, probably being a fever engendered by the insanitary conditions of the town, and not cases of plague. This view is strengthened by the fact that after the middle of the century, when the authorities had completed the paving of the streets and were enforcing sanitary measures, the number of outbreaks was greatly reduced. The worst outbreaks occurred in 1521, 1551, 1556, and 1574.

Oxford may have suffered as much as her sister city, but the town *Records* for the first half of the century were not so fully written. There were outbreaks in 1515, 1551, 1571, 1575, 1592, and 1594. The *Chester Records* give five outbreaks during the century, the worst being in 1551 and 1575. Leicester, Northampton, Nottingham, and Norwich do not report outbreaks until the second half of the century, while Lincoln suffered in 1550 and 1557–58.

It is impossible to ascertain the number of deaths caused

by outbreaks of disease during the first half of the century, for often the scribe recorded some outstanding fact and gave no further information. At Chester, he states that "in three days died ninety-one householders," and at another time "forty died in a night and day." (1) But for the second half of the century a number of town *Records* give almost exact figures, thus making it possible to obtain a good idea of the severity of the outbreaks. In 1574 an outbreak occurred at Cambridge. The students were locked in the colleges, and one of their number died. "Of the townspeople 115 died of the plague from July to the end of November." (2) At Northampton there was an outbreak in 1578, and the deaths for the year rose to one hundred and sixty. As the average number of deaths for the previous five years was sixty-eight, about ninety persons must have died of the plague. (3)

By far the worst outbreak in a provincial town occurred in 1579 at Norwich, a town of about 17,000 people. At the end of June the plague had obtained a firm hold, the deaths averaging fifty weekly. Twice during August the week's total rose above three hundred, with three hundred and fifty during the second week of the month. By the middle of October the number had fallen to two hundred for the week, and continued to fall until in December it was again fifty. Six months later the town was clear, and the returns showed that nearly five thousand people had perished. (4)

As the century advanced the plague appears to have been more widespread; towns that had previously been free were attacked, and the attacks became more deadly. The *Leicester Records* serve admirably to show the growing severity of the attacks, for the Council Meeting Minutes are very complete and can be checked by the Chamberlain's accounts. No mention of plague occurs before 1564. In that year an outbreak is recorded which does not seem to have been serious, and was confined to four houses. Two years later one house was infected, and there was sufficient money remaining from that subscribed for the maintenance of those affected by the previous outbreak to maintain its inhabitants. In 1579 and in 1583 further outbreaks are mentioned, and although no figures are given, it can be seen that each succeeding attack called for a larger amount of money. In 1593 an outbreak occurred that taxed not merely the resources of the town, but also of the county, and in the first five weeks of a six months' attack there were one hundred and seven deaths. (5)

The towns under review did not suffer more than other towns or smaller villages. Newcastle and Manchester provide illustrations. At Newcastle in 1589, in the parish of St. John's, there had been ten deaths before August, in that month there were twenty-two, and three hundred and twenty-four by the end of the year. The *Records* show that 1,727 people died of plague in this outbreak at Newcastle. (6) In 1605 Manchester was but a small manorial village, yet an outbreak of plague there caused about one thousand deaths, and for nearly a year put a stop to all public activity.

If a wider knowledge of town life as revealed by town *Records* refutes the view that towns remained filthy and entirely neglected by ignorant and irresponsible authorities, so must a fuller acquaintance with the little that is known about the origin of the diseases of the sixteenth century modify the opinion that town conditions caused those diseases.

The most feared and most fatal was the "Sweating Sickness" or "Sweat," so called because the first sign of infection was that the victim commenced to sweat profusely. It appeared for the first time in England in 1487, and many *Records* bear witness to its rapid onslaught, describing how persons apparently in the best of health became infected and died within an hour or so. The sudden and fatal nature of the disease, distinguishing it from the plague, earned for it in some places the descriptive names of "Stopgallant" and "New Acquaintances." (7)

Before the end of the fifteenth century it visited many towns twice, and during the sixteenth appeared in 1507,

1517, 1528, and 1550-51. There was nothing to distinguish the outbreak of 1550-51 from previous ones, but with its cessation the "Sweat" vanished, and has not again appeared in England.

Two out of the five outbreaks of disease reported at Chester were the "Sweating Sickness" and caused great loss of life. The outbreak at Cambridge in 1550-51 was—with the possible exception of the "Black Assize" of 1521—the most severe that had befallen the town, and received greater notice because two sons of a former Duke of Suffolk were among the victims. Of six recorded outbreaks of disease at Oxford, two were of the "Sweat," and in the second sixty people died, while at Shrewsbury one of the two outbreaks of pestilence recorded was the "Sweat." The town *Records* show that during the first half of the century, in those towns where outbreaks of disease were recorded, the "Sweat" was the most active and dangerous.

Beyond its mere existence, little was known about the "Sweating Sickness" until modern times. The investigations that have lately been made prove that the disease was introduced into England by hired soldiers that followed the future Henry the Seventh from Picardy into England, and that probably these people acted as germ-carriers and were not themselves affected. Merely a type of low fever in the country of its origin, in England among a susceptible people it developed a fearsome malignant nature. It had, however, one outstanding feature of great importance from the aspect of sanitation: it attacked the well-fed as well as the ill-fed, the rich as well as the poor, the clean places as readily as the dirty. (8)

The recorded particulars of the "Sweating Sickness" are important and interesting. The symptoms of the disease are described in many different town *Records*, and one realizes that it was similar to, if not identical with, the modern influenza. At that time the acknowledged treatment for "Sweating Sickness" was that the victim should go to bed at the first

sign of attack and remain there for four or five days without
exposing even an arm, and as yet no better precaution has
been suggested for its twentieth-century successor. The importance of these facts is apparent. No one would be rash
enough to say that modern influenza is due to bad sanitary
conditions to-day, nor should they imagine that the "Sweating Sickness," one of the most infectious and deadly diseases
of the sixteenth century, was merely a product of bad
sanitary conditions in the towns.

The prisons were another source of disease. These were
crowded by the desperate poor, who because of social and
economic changes were driven to crime for lack of other
means of sustenance. There were also religious and political
prisoners committed by order of the Government, and forgotten until the town grew weary of feeding them. (9) To
these must be added men captured from enemy ships that
were little better than fever dens. In this way disease was
engendered, and at the Assizes the prisoners infected the
people attending the Court, and sometimes most of those
present, judges, jurymen, or visitors, died of the infection.
The Assizes of Cambridge in 1522, of Oxford in 1577, and
of Exeter (10) in 1586 are outstanding instances. At Oxford
about two hundred deaths took place, while from Exeter the
infection spread throughout the county. The full extent of
this kind of "Visitation"—or as it would now be called
typhus epidemic—cannot now be traced, but a contemporary who made a careful study of the disease declared
that "this kind of sickness is one of those rods—and one
of the most common rods—wherewith it pleases God to beat
His people." (11)

Wars then, as ever, were the nursery of disease. Soldiers,
wounded or discharged, were given a sum of money and
left to beg their way across the country to their homes,
carrying and spreading the diseases contracted in camp or
vessel. An incident at Rye will serve to show how dangerous
and costly these troops could be to a town. The Mayor

reported to the Privy Council that there were over eighty soldiers in Rye being supported by the town. After describing their wretched state and how the town had supplied clothes and medicine, he continued: "And now happeneth much to our grief, for persons in whose houses they were lodged, and the women who dieted them have fallen sick, and every day there dies four or five with the infection that they have had from the soldiers." (12)

Apart from the infection, these soldiers had cost the town £55, and were then costing £2 a day, and three months later the Mayor was trying to obtain repayment from the Government officials.

Whatever disease was spread by soldiers in this way was as nothing to the havoc they wrought in another. With the dispersal of the mercenaries employed in the Italian war by Charles the Eighth of France, a disease spread throughout Europe and invaded England with epidemic force. Its ravages were so widespread that one doctor wrote that at one London hospital he treated two hundred cases each year, and that ten out of every twenty cases at another hospital were suffering from this disease. (13) What happened to the thousands of others, ignorant of the nature of the disease and lacking medical advice, can only be guessed.

One other cause of disease must be mentioned. England was an agricultural country with no means of rapid transport, and when the harvest failed in any district it became a famine area. Some of the greatest outbreaks of disease occurred after years of bad harvests, and the question arises: how far was scarcity and bad food a cause of disease? It is well known that damaged rye is a dangerous food, but a medical writer who investigated the causes of some epidemic diseases has declared that as rye was not the staple food of the people, rye-poisoning would not occur to any extent. (14) This view can no longer be maintained. Harrison (1534–93) stated that in his time the rich provided themselves with sufficient wheat, but the poor, even after a good harvest, were usually dependent on rye or barley. (15) This is borne out by the *Records* of the towns. In 1520 the bakers of Leicester were ordered to bake sufficient "rye-bread" for the poor, and when in 1551 the Norwich Council made arrangements to have the market supplied with corn, three hundred and twenty combs of rye were purchased. During three years the Shrewsbury authorities bought one thousand four hundred and sixty quarters of corn, eight hundred of which were rye. (16) *Chester Records* mention only one purchase of corn, and that was rye. For three years the Ipswich authorities spent £600 each year on the purchase of corn, the whole of which, with the exception of one small consignment, was rye. (17) Rye, then, was the staple food of the poor, and in bad seasons would probably be damaged. At such times private supplies were held back in order to obtain higher prices, and storage would increase its dangerous properties. A contemporary writer had no doubts about the disastrous consequences of using bad corn. "Farmers," he said, "in hopes of getting higher prices, stored their corn until it had gone bad" . . . "yet being the only supply it had even then to be eaten" . . . "whereby many thousands of all degrees are consumed, by whose deaths in my opinion they are not unguilty." (18)

So it will be seen that in addition to the "Sweating Sickness" a number of other diseases were prevalent, taking their toll of life and creating problems that had to be dealt with by the towns. Yet their causes were not rooted in town conditions, nor could they be prevented by any action the town authorities could take.

NOTES

1. Morris, *Chester*, 64, 65.
2. Cooper, *Cambridge*, ii. 322–324.
3. *Northampton Records*, ii. 233–238.
4. *Norwich Records*, ii. p. cxxvi.
5. *Leicester Records*, iii. 112, 120, 179, 193, 291.
6. Welford, *Newcastle and Gateshead*, iii. 56.
7. Creighton, *Epidemics in Britain*, i. 260, 262.
8. *Ibid.*, i. 269–79.
9. *Rye, Hist. MSS. Comm. Report* 13, App. Part iv. 82.
10. Jenkins, *History of Exeter*, 126.
11. Cogham, *Haven of Health*, 319.
12. *Rye, Hist. MSS. Comm. Report* 13. App. iv. 92, 95.
13. Clowes, *Profitable Book of Observation*, 149–150.
14. Creighton, *Epidemics in Britain*, i. 53.
15. Harrison, *Description of England*, i. 153. (Furnival.)
16. *Shrewsbury, Hist. MSS. Comm. Report* 15. App. Part x. 61.
17. Bacon, *Ipswiche*, 381, 387.
18. Harrison, *Description of England*, i. 299. (Furnival.)

CHAPTER XVI

DEALING WITH THE PLAGUE

By whatever means infection was introduced, the town had to deal with the outbreak, and experience soon taught the people that in the case of the plague the danger arose through the arrival of persons and goods from infected areas. Dr. Perne, a Vice-Chancellor of Cambridge University, in a letter to Lord Burghley, writes that "they must agree that the first cause is sin," and then goes on, "but so far as I understand it is not the corruption of the air as the physicians say, but partly by the apparel of one that came from London and died in Barnwell, where the plague is now most vehement." (1) This man had come to the "Midsummer Fair," and these great fairs that were attended by traders with goods from all over the country were regarded as one of the ways by which the plague was spread from town to town.

To forgo a fair or close its markets would mean a heavy financial loss to a town, or even cause some scarcity of provisions, so only after careful consideration would authorities decide that a market or fair should not be held. Yet some authorities adopted the policy. In 1592 Shrewsbury closed its wool market, and ordered that no wool, flax, household stuff, or wearing apparel, should be brought from London or any other infected town, and to enforce the regulations placed men to guard every gate of the town. (2) The Exeter authorities, because the plague was active in London, announced that "the Fair of Saint Nicholas is deferred and there is no Fair at all this time" . . . "for by fairs may the same be spread, and places now free, infected." (3) Hastings, also fearing the plague might be brought there from London, decided that its fair should not be held.

Citizens were forbidden to visit the markets and fairs of

infected towns. No inhabitant of Shrewsbury was "to go to the city of London or other place infected with the plague," or if having done so, was "not to return within four miles of the town before two months be ended." (4) When an outbreak occurred at Derby the citizens of Nottingham were forbidden to visit the town, and "Inn-keepers and Tipplers" were ordered to refuse admittance to any person from Derby.

The regulations were enforced. At Nottingham the inhabitants had been forbidden to visit "Lenton Fair" under the penalty of being "shut up and disfranchised," and to see the regulations were observed it was decided to keep "watchers" at various places on the road and appoint "some honest men to go to Lenton" to see if any of the inhabitants disobeyed the order.

To close the market or abandon the annual fair would not commend itself to the trading section of the community if it was thought possible to continue without great risk of infection. During an outbreak at Leicester in 1593 the county Justices of the Peace advised the Mayor to close the market, but the Town Council thought their precautions were sufficient to prevent further infection, and continued the market throughout the attack. The Oxford authorities were "very anxious about people coming from infected places, but fear that stopping the fair will cause murmers among the King's people." They therefore held the "Frideswide Fair," but announced that none from London would be admitted without a "permit" as being free from infection. This was a common custom. The Bridgnorth authorities, in a letter to the Shrewsbury Council, stated that as there were rumours that Shrewsbury had the plague, "all persons from that town who wished to attend Bridgnorth Fair must have a certificate that they and their families were free from plague." (5)

Restrictions were placed on the transfer of goods, people being forbidden to bring anything from London or other

infected places into towns that were free. This was a necessary precaution. A man at Nottingham was fined for receiving goods "that came from the sickness, whereby he put
the whole town in jeopardy." These goods were sent by his
son, who was the caretaker of an infected house in another
town, and may have been the property of persons who had
died of the plague.

Other methods were also adopted to keep the town free
from infection. People fled from infected districts hoping
to find some place free from the scourge, but as they often
carried the germs of the disease, town authorities took precautions against their entry. In walled towns this was easy:
men were placed at the gates "for the oversight of those
who shall come to the town," or "to watch the town and
stay the people from the infected places." At Newcastle-
on-Tyne, at a period when infection was feared, the Council
ordered the coalminers "to make their homes outside the
walls so that it would not be necessary to open the gates
at the early hour they went to work." (6) How careful a
watch was kept is seen from the *Shrewsbury Records*, for sixpence was given to a man who brought information that
an infected woman was travelling toward the town, and the
next item is that three shillings and twopence was paid to
the persons who met and conducted her past the town. (7)
At Nottingham a small sum was given to "a poor man that
was suspected to have the plague to leave the town," and
a citizen "presented" for receiving his sister, "knowing the
visitation to be in the town in which she dwelt."

The regulations were harsh, but the towns could not deal
with people from other places, and must be judged by the
standards of the age. In times of distress those who should
have led the fight fled to country retreats, and from these
havens gave advice to others. At the outbreak of plague in
1563 the Queen retired to Windsor, and drastic measures
were taken to prevent infection reaching there. A gallows
was erected in the market-place, and on it "without any

K

judgment" were hung all those that came from London by road, as well as those who attempted to convey goods between the two places by water. (8) Harsh as the treatment of the man at Nottingham may appear, he received aid from the town, whereas he might have received a halter from the Queen.

Nearly all the town regulations indicate that London was known to be the chief source of infection. The two greatest outbreaks of plague at Cambridge were the result of direct infection from London. (9) "The plague was twice in Oxford within twelve years, being brought from London both times," (10) and the greatest and most fatal of all provincial outbreaks—that at Norwich—commenced with people from London who had followed the Queen when she visited Norwich. (11) A careful study of town *Records* leads to the conclusion that modern ideas of the plague have been formed from references to London outbreaks. London was often the scene of disastrous outbreaks and a source of infection to the rest of the country. Further, there is no indication that the City rulers understood how infectious diseases should be controlled. This does not apply to the provincial towns, where during the sixteenth century the authorities evolved a system of control.

There was little national regulation to help the town in the fight against disease. In 1488, as a result of the prevalence of "Sweating Sickness," an order was issued which forbade the killing of cattle within the town. At that time cattle were killed in the autumn and the flesh salted for use during the winter, so the conditions may have been very insanitary. Probably for military reasons, Berwick and Carlisle were excepted from this order. (12)

The next plague order was in 1518. During this outbreak the Court retired to the country, and from its retreat Sir Thomas More wrote to the Mayor of Oxford, where a slight outbreak had occurred, giving instructions on behalf of the King. The Mayor was ordered to keep the infected people within their houses, and persons who had been in contact with them were to carry white rods when in the streets. (13) A further order followed in 1543. This was more detailed and formed the basis of succeeding regulations during the century. Houses that had been infected had to be marked by a cross for forty days after a death, and if the survivors had sufficient means to subsist without working they were to remain indoors. If, however, they were without means they were to carry white rods as they went about their work. Straw that had been used as bedding had to be burnt at night and clothing put out in the fields to air. A further provision was that hounds, spaniels, mastiffs, and all valuable dogs were to be taken out of the town and others destroyed. (14)

The rest of the orders down to 1593 are special London regulations. In 1563 the people were ordered to make fires in the streets at night to drive away the pestilential vapours, and the authorities were to appoint persons who during outbreaks could supply closed houses with food. In addition steps had to be taken to support those infected persons who could not maintain themselves. Further measures followed in 1581, when "Searchers" were appointed to "view" the dead, and to certify the cause of death, so that the extent of the outbreaks could be registered.

Two publications dealing with the plague outbreak of 1592–93 have been known, but a third, issued in 1593, is of greater value because it was an attempt by the Queen and Privy Council to bring to the notice of the people everything then known about the plague. It is in two sections, one dealing with the regulations to be enforced during an outbreak, and the other "Advice by the best learned physicians of the Realm, containing sundry good rules and easy medicines without charge to the meaner sort of people."

The regulations command the Justices of the Peace to take charge of any outbreak of plague, and describe the financial and other arrangements that were to be made to control the outbreaks and secure the maintenance of the infected people. The clothes of these people had to be disinfected or destroyed, and a register kept of all deaths. In church-yard and market-place notices had to be displayed which gave particulars of the preventives and remedies suggested by the physicians. Special instructions are given as to en-forcing isolation and for the burial of the dead.

The last two items are important. The age was one of strong religious feeling, and to the people isolation had a religious aspect. Was it in keeping with Christian charity to refuse to mix with the suffering people? "Many believed it was wrong to do so, and this cost them their lives." (15) But religious beliefs were not allowed to stand in the way when combating disease. Care had to be taken that no "person of the meanest state" was left unprovided for, but intercourse between infected and others had to cease. If "lay" persons because of religious beliefs persisted in mixing with infected people they were to be imprisoned, if "curates" did so they were to be reprimanded and forbidden to preach. The other item is important, for a medical writer has said that almost the only thing left undone that might have been of service in combating the plague was the burial of the dead away from the town. (16) This the regulation ordered to be done, and towns made arrangements for it.

The second part of the book deals with the cause of the plague, and suggests medicines and methods of treatment. In accordance with the custom of the time, sin was said to be the primary cause. Subsidiary causes were "foul air from moors and fens, standing water and ditches, channels and mixens, and multitudes of people living in small rooms uncleanly kept." For the purification of houses, or as a personal preventive, vinegar was regarded as the sovereign remedy. (17)

Whatever is thought of these opinions, the instructions for the care of the patient command respect. Diet was all-im-portant. At the end of the nineteenth century a specialist who had made a study of the plague published his conclusions for the benefit of medical people working in the East. It is interesting to note that unknown to himself he was just repeating the advice his predecessors had given three hundred years earlier. (18)

NOTES

1. Cooper, *Cambridge*, ii. 322.
2. Owen and Blakeway, *Shrewsbury*, i. 397.
3. *Exeter, Hist. MSS. Comm. Report*, 310.
4. Owen and Blakeway, *Shrewsbury*, i. 354.
5. *Ibid.*, i. 368.
6. Welford, *Newcastle and Gateshead*, ii. 385.
7. Owen and Blakeway, *Shrewsbury*, i. 399.
8. *Three Fifteenth-Century Chronicles* (Camden Society), 127.
9. Cooper, *Cambridge*, ii. 375.
10. Cogham, *Haven of Health*, 296.
11. *Norwich Records*, ii. p. cxxv.
12. *Statutes*, ii. 527.
13. *Oxford Records*, 18.
14. Creighton, *Epidemics in Britain*, i. 315, 319.
15. Cooper, *Cambridge*, ii. 323.
16. Creighton, *Epidemics in Britain*, i. 331, 336.
17. Orders thought meet by Her Majesty and Her Privy Council for the preservation of Her good subjects from the Plague.
18. Cantile, *The Plague. How to Recognize, Prevent and Treat*, 60.

CHAPTER XVII

THE ISOLATION HOSPITAL

AT present, when a doctor is consulted in almost every illness, and when an authoritative certificate must be secured
to permit burial, early warning is received of the arrival
of any infectious diseases. No such conditions existed in the
sixteenth century. However careful the authorities might be
to prevent the plague or other disease gaining an extrance
into the town, it could be firmly established before they were
aware of its existence. An entry in the register of the Holy
Trinity Church at Chester illustrates this fact. In the list of
burials is one entry, "Alice, daughter of James Hind, buried
at the Church." "The first that died of plague in the parish,
but was not known to the parish till she was buried." The
town *Records* show that for the following four months the
plague raged at Chester. (1)

The anxiety of the authorities and the methods adopted
to secure early information can be seen from the *Gloucester*
and *Shrewsbury Records*. At Gloucester, any householder having
a sick person in his house for twenty-four hours "must
declare the same to the Mayor, and what he thinks of it
upon his burgess oath." (2) At Shrewsbury two women were
sent by the authorities "to search a girl" and report on her
illness. (3)

When the infection had shown itself, the usual course was
to command infected persons to stay in their houses for
some definite length of time. At Leicester no person was
"to go abroad amongst them that be clear, within two
months after any shall chance to die of the plague in their
house," under a penalty of £5. (4) Norwich, Lincoln, Cambridge, and Shrewsbury had similar regulations. The period
of isolation thought necessary varied, and in one outbreak
Nottingham thought that twenty days were sufficient. At

Lincoln, the Aldermen were made responsible for seeing
that the orders were obeyed, and at Shrewsbury the authorities paid an individual to watch and prevent infected people
leaving their houses.

It must not be assumed that this method of isolation was
easy to enforce, for it was really against the spirit of the
times. "Some believe that one ought not to shun another
Christian that is infected, and as a result, unless God un-
naturally interferes, the infection is spread, and some who
did this are dead and all their household." (5)

No doubt stern measures were used to compel obedience
to the regulations, and at Cambridge people were marched
through the streets to prison for "not keeping the order."
A week later these people were tried, some were heavily
fined, and the rest, perhaps too poor to pay any fine, were
sent back to spend another night in prison. (6)

To control the plague successfully, more stringent measures
were necessary, and the first hint of real compulsion comes
from Gloucester, where the accounts contain an item "For
paling in the sick folk in St. Michael's parish." Though not
generally adopted, this method of securing isolation by in-
closing the infected area with a fence was tried with great
success at Leicester, and during a long outbreak the market
was kept going and the Assizes held in the town. So thorough
were the authorities there, that not only were the infected
people isolated, but also those who had been in contact with
them.

The town authorities were anxious that persons who had
been in contact with the infected people should not mix
with the rest of the inhabitants, even though the national
regulations permitted them to do so. It could, however, only
be prevented by providing sufficient food to maintain them
in isolation. Each town in its own way tried to do this,
and that they succeeded can be seen from a statement
by the Vice-Chancellor of Cambridge University, "that
one thing spreads the plague is that the poor, seeing the

good provision made for the infected, wish the same to continue." (7)

The method of isolating the infected families and houses made it necessary to have someone in charge, so keepers were appointed to reside in the houses, and others were engaged to deliver the food and other requirements. The position of keeper in an infected house could not have been desirable, but then, as ever, people were willing to face the risks, and women, after seeing their own children provided for, went to live in the houses of the plague-stricken. No one is likely to say that the "16d paid to Inglyshes wife for keeping Kyichames house, being visited with the plague for ten weeks," was not well earned. (8)

An incident at Winchester arising out of the need for keepers is worth recording. In 1583 the authorities decided that "there shall be appointed eight women to be vergers or nurses of such houses as be suspected of infection, and they shall have weekly until the infection cease . . ., and after the infection weekly . . ., and a convenient place to be provided for the said women, by the Mayor and his Brethren." If carried out, this regulation would have secured the establishment of a nursing-home, with a staff of nurses in attendance. Unfortunately no further information is given in the *Records*. (9)

A London Proclamation had ordered the authorities to appoint persons in each ward to "view" the dead, and thus enable the number of deaths from plague to be recorded. This was regarded as being women's work, and at Northampton two were appointed and paid twenty pence per week, but Norwich employed a man both to "search" and record the names of the victims.

A regulation enforced almost everywhere required that owners should kill or remove their dogs out of the town at the beginning of an outbreak of disease, and in most places cats were to be destroyed. No one thought of rats causing infection, but there was a general belief that domestic animals in some way spread the disease, and an outbreak at Oxford in which a family of eleven lost their lives was said to be caused by an infected fur bought in London. (10)

When the infection was known to be in the town, the authorities, as at Shrewsbury, ordered "that all swine and dogs be avoided out of the town on pain of forfeiture"; and after the warning had been given, all animals found in the street were killed and their owners fined. The order must have been enforced very quickly, for at Newcastle, after the bellman "had been about the town to warn all men to keep up their swine and dogs," a butcher went around and later had to be paid for killing "five swine, twenty-four dogs, and sixteen ducks, found in the streets after warning had been given." (11) Town authorities maintained a free medical service for the poor, but in times of pestilence they did their best to secure additional aid. At Cambridge the authorities wrote to the Bishop of Lincoln "concerning a man that should cure the visited," and later "William the Surgeon" was brought to the town to advise what action could best be taken; (12) and the *Records* of Norwich, Liverpool, and Rye show that extra aid was given. But no real measure of isolation could be secured by regulations that allowed those in contact with the infected to go about the streets, and this accounts for the fact that in London the plague was never brought under control. The town authorities realized this, but so little has been known of the inner life of sixteenth-century towns that a suggestion by an eighteenth-century writer concerning the desirability of municipal isolation hospitals was recently noted as marking a great advance on former ideas of treatment, whereas in reality the suggested method had been in practice in provincial towns one hundred and fifty years earlier. (13)

In 1558 the Liverpool authorities announced that in future "all persons infected with the pestilence" . . . "shall depart out of their houses and make their cabins on the heath." This regulation was only to be enforced in the summer.

During winter infected persons were to remain in their houses, "to keep their doors and windows shut on the street side until they have licence from the Mayor to open them, and their houses to be cleaned, dressed, and dyght with such as be appointed."

The following year the scheme was put into operation, and Elyn Denton was ordered to "avoid the town to some convenient place with all expedition, until God send her health." (14) No further cases are recorded, so probably the measures proved effective.

Huts, some distance from the town, would be difficult to warm and provision during the winter, which may account for that part of the scheme being restricted to the summer. This seems likely, for almost a century later Northampton authorities decided "that as winter was coming on, it was not feasible to set up a pest-house remote from the town," and so used a tower on the city wall for the purpose. (15)

Within a few years the public had realized the advantage of removing infected people. A slight outbreak occurred at Chester, and in accordance with the ordinary practice the sufferers were ordered to remain indoors. A little later a letter was received by the Mayor from the inhabitants of Pepper Street, where the infected people lived, protesting that their lives and the City were in danger, "because the infected people will not obey orders." They asked the Mayor "to remove the infected people to some other convenient place until God restore them to their former health." (16) How wide the idea had spread can be seen from the various *Records*. The *Nottingham Records* show that in 1575 a case of plague was isolated for a month, and this was repeated the following year. In neither instance were there further cases.

Meantime the idea of complete isolation was put into operation at Cambridge. In 1574 plague broke out, and the Vice-Chancellor and the Mayor collaborated to gain control of the outbreak. It was agreed that the infected people should be isolated, and for the purpose a piece of land known as the Old Clay Pits was to be utilized. It is only from the accounts that particulars can be obtained. The land was levelled at a cost of £3 12s., and a further £14 18s. 4d. was spent on enclosing the area with a ditch. No idea of the size of the place is given, but the money would employ about twenty men for a month in levelling and ditching. Then on material for the house and for providing a bridge across the ditch a further £3 6s. 8d. was spent. This was probably the first fever isolation hospital built by a local authority. From the accounts it appears to have been a wood frame house, with wattle daubed sides and a thatched roof, the whole costing £21 17s. (17)

The idea of providing buildings outside the town to isolate the infected people gradually spread. The Newcastle accounts in 1576 give a sum "paid for the sick folk afield this week," (18) and in 1587 the Leicester authorities declared their intention "to build a convenient house for such as be visited to inhabit during the time of such visitation," but they did not carry out their intention at the time. In 1603 the register of Holy Trinity Church at Chester records the deaths from plague of people who "died at the cabins." (19) Northampton secured a building known as the College "to be used as a pest-house," and in 1603 paid 40s. as compensation to the owner. (20) The *Oxford, Manchester*, and *Nottingham Records* show that the method was accepted as the proper procedure. At Oxford in 1593 people were isolated on a common some distance from the town. At Nottingham in 1604 cabins "had to be built at the cost of the town," and in the following year, when letting a piece of land outside the town, the authorities preserved the right to erect isolation cabins on one part, if they were needed. Six years later they paid compensation for a place "being occupied by the visited folk." Manchester made similar provision. "Collehurste," a common over which freemen had rights, was about one mile from the town, and because of the distance the citizens agreed to lease the land for £10 per year, the money to go to the poor-box, "providing that in time of infection, the inhabitants can lawfully build cabins on six acres nearest to the town, and there bury their dead if need be." (21)

Was this method of isolation merely temporary, or persisted in for a long time? The *Oxford Records* show that it was both thorough and continuous. Isolation places are mentioned for the first time in 1593, in connection with an outbreak in which a visitor from London was the first to die of the plague. Two years later one house was infected and the inmates were removed to the place of isolation. In the following year a death was reported at the isolation centre, but no other cases were mentioned. In 1603 there was an outbreak, and all infected persons were removed and isolated. Three years later three children in one house died suddenly, and as the authorities feared that plague might be the cause, they isolated those remaining in the house, also the household of the woman who had prepared the bodies for burial. A serious outbreak of plague followed, and the infected people were isolated in cabins. In 1608 the Council asked two women to bury the body of a girl, and arranged that afterwards these women should be isolated until it was seen if they had been infected. Again an outbreak followed, and £20 was spent on isolation huts. Then for a long time the town remained free from infection, the next outbreak being in 1624. This was the worst attack experienced by the town, but the authorities decided that every infected person must be isolated, and the accounts show that £73 was spent on cabins. (22) From this it will be seen that for over thirty years, whether the outbreak was confined to one house or spread over the town, every known case was isolated.

So during the century the idea of isolating infectious diseases was developed and carried to a practical conclusion by some of the provincial towns.

NOTES

1. Farral, *Holy Trinity Parish Church Register*, 70.
2. *Gloucester, Hist. MSS. Comm. Report* 12, App. Part ix. 460.
3. Owen and Blakeway, *Shrewsbury*, i. 321.
4. *Leicester Records*, iii. 110.
5. Cooper, *Cambridge*, ii. 322.
6. *Ibid.*, ii. 110.
7. *Ibid.*, ii. 322.
8. *Leicester Records*, iii. 112.
9. Bailey, *Winchester*, 107.
10. Creighton, *Epidemics in Britain*, i. 316.
11. Welford, *Newcastle and Gateshead*, ii. 385.
12. Cooper, *Cambridge*, ii. 523.
13. Morris, *The Story of English Public Health*, 15.
14. Picton, *Liverpool Records*, 93, 94.
15. *Northampton Records*, ii. 239.
16. Morris, *Chester*, 79.
17. Cooper, *Cambridge*, ii. 321.
18. Welford, *Newcastle and Gateshead*, ii. 486.
19. Farral, *Holy Trinity Parish Church Register*, 70, 71.
20. *Northampton Records*, ii. 237.
21. *Manchester Records*, ii. 311.
22. Salter, *Oxford Council Acts*, 80, 92, 153, 173–174, 186, 331, 376, 400.

CHAPTER XVIII

THE COST OF THE PLAGUE

Town authorities found the maintenance of infected people no easy task, but realized that if isolation was to be enforced the cost had to be met. Some idea of the burden imposed on a town can be gained from the reports of the Leicester outbreak of 1593. The first mention of the infection was at a Council meeting in September, when it was decided that "the Twenty-four (Aldermen) shall pay weekly towards the visited folks, 2/- each,—the Forty-eight—(Councillors) 1/- each." By November 4th twenty-one houses were "visited" and thirty-five persons had died, and the deaths increased to one hundred and seven by the twenty-eighth of the month. "All visited houses are kept supplied with meat, fire, drink, candles, and soap, and provided with keepers." In a letter to the County Justices asking for help, the Mayor stated that they had to maintain between five and six hundred people, for all those who had been in contact with the infection were isolated. In addition to the keepers twenty men were employed to prevent any person breaking through the cordon drawn round the infected places.

In November the heavy charges, with the fear of the infection, were causing some of the inhabitants to remove, and the Council decided that "those who leave the town and do not return nightly to their dwelling houses, to pay double charges; and those who continue out after Our Lady Day next, shall pay for every day they continue out, 40/- towards the charges of the visited." The plague continued until March of the following year, and the cost of the outbreak must have been a crushing burden for the four thousand inhabitants. (1)

To raise money, most town authorities adopted their usual methods of taxation. At Leicester, where the town was governed by a Council of twenty-four Aldermen and forty-eight Councillors, it was customary to divide the amount required into three parts, one part to be borne by the Aldermen, the second by the Councillors, and the third part, "assessed on the inhabitants by the Mayor and other Justices, everyone according to their ability." Thus the individual contribution of an Alderman was always double that of a Councillor. In 1554 a levy of 5s. each was paid by the Aldermen, and one of 2s. 6d. by the Councillors; the total contribution by the rest of the inhabitants being £5 14s. 4d. (2)

There was always an attempt to distribute the burden as equitably as possible. When a large sum of money was needed during the outbreak at Norwich in 1579, the Council decided that the Aldermen should each pay £1, and past and present Sheriffs 13s. 4d. The Aldermen were also to divide the "commons" into three groups, the best sort to pay 10s., the second sort 5s., and the third 2s. 6d. each. At Oxford each member of the "thirteen" (the Aldermen) was to pay sixteenpence, Chamberlains and Common Councillors eightpence each, "and of every commoner and others that are able, at the least fourpence; the same to be paid monthly."

Lincoln's arrangement was simple. Every Alderman was requested to pay fourpence weekly, "and every other person of ability twopence each week." The authorities at Ipswich at first depended upon the poor-rate assessment. At the beginning of one outbreak those paying weekly towards the poor were called upon "to pay at once a month's rate, and yet continue paying as before." Finding this would not suffice, £100 was granted from the town funds, "and should this be insufficient, the inhabitants shall be assessed as be thought needful." Later it was realized that the poor-rate was not a suitable source of revenue for these occasional charges, and it was decided that in future the money should be raised on the same assessment as the subsidy, with the addition "that every inhabitant not liable to the subsidy should also be charged."

Sometimes infected families were maintained by friends, and wealthy people were expected to support themselves. At Oxford the maintenance of a shoemaker and his family cost the town £10, and later the authorities claimed that he was able to repay them. They were willing to accept one-third of this sum, but the man refused to pay anything and was committed to prison. (3)

Few towns could have maintained an organized fight against the disease without help from outside. How readily this was given is shown by the *Shrewsbury Records*. During an outbreak there in 1576 Mr. Price, a former inhabitant, wrote to the Mayor stating that he had heard there was a great scarcity of corn in the town, and offered the authorities his own store at the "County price." He also offered to lend £20 or £40 to buy supplies elsewhere. Wishing to help the town further, he advised the Mayor to write asking the "Vice-President of Wales" to aid the town in its time of need. This advice was followed, and the Vice-President ended a sympathetic reply with "and as for your markets if any want be, let me understand, and that which the counties do yield in victuals or other, I will send to your town daily, as you shall warn me or send me word." (4)

There is little reason to doubt that many towns, having themselves experienced the dangers and difficulties of an attack, gave practical expression to their sympathy for a stricken town. An incident at Rye illustrates this. During an outbreak of disease the Mayor received a donation of £5 from the inhabitants of Ashford, "they had had the plague and found many friends"—"so now they send help in return."

Sending food was as helpful as sending money, and a quotation from the *Nottingham Records* shows how this was given. During an outbreak in 1592 there was received between the 8th and the 22nd of August:—

In money, in sums from 5/– to 40/–	£4	0	0
120 lbs of Bacon, 20 Cheeses, 1 Bacon Flitch, and			
12 strike of Corn, and 4 Strike of Corn		40	0
20 Strike of Rye and 20 of Malt, and		16	8
6 Strike of Corn, and		40	0
1 Bullock, and 5 Quarters of Rye			
4 Quarters of Wheat and 8 Quarters of Malt			

In the following week goods and money continued to be received, among other items being £4 10s. sent by the County Justices. (5)

So although sometimes the town could finance itself, when this was impossible it could depend upon outside aid, and it can be maintained that in the provincial town the victims of plague or other infectious diseases were well cared for.

NOTES

1. *Leicester Records*, iii. 293–295.
2. *Ibid.*, p. xxx.
3. Salter, *Oxford Council Acts*, 162.
4. Owen and Blakeway, *Shrewsbury*, 369–370.
5. *Nottingham Records*, iv. 238.

CHAPTER XIX

WHEN A TOWN AUTHORITY FAILED

IN concluding the survey of town regulations for the control of disease, it seems desirable to examine more closely the outbreak that took place at Norwich in 1579. This was so disastrous that of a population of 17,000 nearly 5,000 died.

Since no other outbreak of so fatal a nature had taken place in any other provincial town, the question arises, Was Norwich in a worse sanitary condition, or was it more lax in its plague restrictions? It has already been said that Leicester enforced restrictions so well that it was possible to hold the market and the Assize Court without any great danger during a very bad outbreak. So why did Norwich fail? It has been stated that the plague resulted from infection due to a Royal visit. This took place in August, and at the Council meetings there is no mention of the outbreak before the following March, when it was reported to be in two parishes. (1)

The townspeople attributed the outbreak to the dirty habits of the foreign settlers who were numerous in the town. Refugees from the Netherlands had commenced to arrive in the town in 1565, (2) and during the following seven years nearly 4,000 settled there. (3) By the year of the plague their number had risen to 6,000. (4) The charges against them were very severe; they were said to have filthy houses, to corrupt the river by washing cloth, and to allow the channels of the streets to become filthy. These charges were probably true. The foreigners were mostly confined to one portion of the town, and it would have been almost impossible for the town to absorb 6,000 people in fourteen years without overcrowding and its attendant evils.

The orders issued by the Mayor were directed to the foreigners, commanding them to adopt better sanitary methods and "to use the fumes and preservatives recommended by the physicians." Nothing more is recorded for three months, and then the plague had gained the mastery, the deaths averaging fifty per week. Orders were then issued that persons from infected houses were not to go out for six weeks; money was provided to maintain the poor, and an official appointed to register the deaths from plague. During the period that followed, when the deaths rose at one time to over three hundred per week, formal orders of the Council were not to be expected, and none appeared until the following March. Then instructions were given that infected houses were to be marked by a paper bearing the words "Lord have mercy on us" attached to the door. People from infected houses were to carry a white rod when in the street and not attend public meetings. A further instruction that no household goods were to be sold without the Mayor's consent was a very necessary precaution, for many houses would be desolate, and the distribution of the goods likely to cause further infection.

When the epidemic had ceased, the full extent of its ravages could be seen. Almost half of the alien population and one in five of the natives had been carried off. Further, the disease was chiefly confined to the poorer people, and not one of the twenty-four Aldermen died.

There are exceptional features about this outbreak. First, nearly six months elapsed before the authorities took action, and almost another three before they followed the usual practice of providing funds to maintain the infected people. But the most outstanding thing was that at the Council meeting before the last plague order was issued the Council members pledged themselves, if necessary, (5) to protect the Mayor for issuing and enforcing the regulations. These were only weak and similar to those usually issued in London, and lacked the vigour of the provincial town's usual restrictions, so whom could the authorities fear? The explanation is probably to be found in the foreign element. Although the foreigners greatly increased the prosperity of Norwich, there was considerable friction between them and the town authorities, who in accordance with the custom of the time tried to control their trading activities. (6) Freer trading rights were conceded in 1571, but for a long time the foreigners must have remained a community separated by customs and language from the natives. (7) As the plague commenced amongst the aliens, the town authorities may have been reluctant to interfere at the beginning of the outbreak, and the fearful death-roll was the result.

NOTES

1. *Norwich Records*, ii. 335.
2. Lipson, *Economic History of England*, i. 435.
3. *Norwich Records*, ii. p. lxxxiii.
4. Lipson, *Economic History of England*, i. 435.
5. *Norwich Records*, ii. 189.
6. Lipson, *Economic History of England*, i. 435, 436.
7. Cunningham, *Industry and Commerce—Modern Times*, Part i. 83, 84.

CHAPTER XX

CONCLUSION

In the previous pages it has been shown that the town authorities in the sixteenth century attempted to enforce the cleaning of streets, to secure supplies of pure water, and to remove or prevent anything happening to prejudice the health of the people. It has also been made clear that much of the disease of the time did not arise out of town conditions, and it should be remembered that there are no known changes in the sanitary conditions of the country to account for the disappearance of the "Sweating Sickness" in 1551 and of the plague just over a century later. It is also certain that the virulence of some of the diseases was due not to faulty sanitation, but to the fact that the infected people lacked the power of resistance which seems to be engendered by exposure to repeated attacks, and which was possessed by the people in the place where the disease was originated.

In their treatment of plague outbreaks some town authorities left little to be desired, for the method of removing infected people to places outside the town is still the approved method of securing isolation during outbreaks of infectious diseases. The opinion—expressed by a medical writer after a long investigation into the causes of infectious diseases—that the only safeguard that might have been tried was to bury in some places outside the town those who had died of the plague is splendid testimony to the activities of the authorities. (1) But the town *Records* prove this was done, so what further criticism can be advanced?

As it is interesting to know something of these towns at a later date, their condition in the middle of the nineteenth century may be briefly reviewed. The particulars given are from the reports published in 1844–45 by a Royal Commission which had been investigating the sanitary condition of a number of towns. (2)

The first great change noticed is in the size of the towns. The 17,000 inhabitants of Norwich had grown to 62,000. Leicester had 50,000 instead of 4,000, Coventry 31,000, and the small sixteenth-century village of Liverpool had become a town of 223,000 inhabitants.

The housing of these had altered the design of the town. Gardens had disappeared, and in their place, within the squares formed by the original houses, other squares of houses had been built until the whole area had been covered. (3) These squares, or courts as they are called, "Were clustered upon each other, court within court, yard within yard, and lane within lane." So close were the houses that it was not possible to have a proper road into the courts, and yards and houses could only be reached by means of a narrow tunnel passing through one of the blocks of houses. (4) This method of housing was common to all the towns, but in a few instances extra accommodation had been secured by utilizing cellar dwellings, and in Liverpool one-sixth of the people lived in "underground cellars." (5)

How many persons live in one house? This was a question often asked by the Commissioners. At Liverpool the average was seven, with areas in which it was fifteen. (6) At Norwich it was frequent to find four or five families in one house, or ten persons to each room. (7) At Shrewsbury "one family usually occupied a house, but in one suburb, half the poor live two or more families in a house." (8) This compares unfavourably with Norwich in 1570. Then in one of the poorest districts of the town and in the poorest homes the average was but 3·5. (9)

The paving and cleaning of the streets and the removal of refuse were questions to which the Commissioners gave great attention, but in not one of the towns where previously the inhabitants had to pave and keep clean the space before their doors was there any regulation to enforce the paving or sweeping of the streets. In one or two places the main street was swept occasionally by paupers, (10) but for those miles of streets, courts, and yards wherein the thousands lived not the slightest sanitary regulation existed. The authorities have now no power over side streets. (11) Contrast this against conditions at Northampton at an earlier period. In 1609 a lane was reported to be "dirty and noisome," so the owners or occupiers of lands or tenements adjoining were ordered to repair the same "in such manner as shall be prescribed by the Chamberlain" under a penalty of 40s. each.

In the sixteenth century it was an offence to throw rubbish in the street, and the aid of the citizens had been enlisted to detect offenders. In the middle of the nineteenth century it was the accepted method of disposal. No matter how vile the filth, it was thrown into the street, to remain until the accumulation induced someone to cart it away for manure. (12)

The inhabitants were not to blame, for over and over again the street was said to be the only available place to deposit rubbish. One example is sufficient. In one town nearly 9,000 houses inhabited by 60,000 people were without ashpit, convenience, or one inch of ground on which to deposit filth, which therefore of necessity had to be thrown into the street. (13) There was now no thought of inspection, and the sixteenth-century "scavenger" with his cart would be useless, for the filth had become private property. (14)

There is also the question of the water supply. The Commissioners say "it does not appear to be a generally recognized principle, that it should form part of the duty of a body governing the town, to provide an adequate supply of water." (15) At Chester, where a plentiful supply was provided in the sixteenth century, a portion of the town was supplied three or four times a week, while the rest of the people had to drink water carried from the river or canal. (16) Coventry was short of water. The old conduit and the right to supply the town had passed into the hands of a private company. At Shrewsbury a few houses were supplied on three days each week, and three days' supply had to be stored at the week-end. The majority of the people had to carry water from the river, or buy from those who brought it round in barrels. Leicester's 50,000 people depended upon the sixteenth-century conduit, (17) and at Norwich, where once the town authority owned a fine water works and supplied water twice a day, the supply was in private hands; water was only supplied to one quarter of the town, and "the rest have often to steal it." (18) Nottingham alone of all the towns had a plentiful supply, and that from two private companies. (19)

The importance of town drainage had been forgotten. Leicester had a death-rate of thirty per thousand "due to lack of drainage." (20) In Coventry the earlier authorities had always insisted that the River Sherbourne should be kept clean and free from obstruction, but now its course was choked by dams and become so foul a nuisance that the people begged and the Commissioners recommended that these be removed and the water allowed to flow freely.

Nothing reveals better the changed conception of town sanitation at the two periods than the attitude toward pig-keeping within the town. In the sixteenth century in a small village the inhabitants protested against the action of a person who had a pig but no proper sty, and at once the authorities made regulations to prevent any nuisance or danger to health arising through pig-keeping. In the middle of the nineteenth century, not only were "pigs, asses and poultry kept in living houses," (21) but rows of houses were built with pigsties in the basement.

At Nottingham "fevers were traced to houses where pigs were kept in cellars," and "holes in the rocks served as combined piggeries and dairies." (22) The change can best be seen by contrasting Birmingham with Coventry. At the latter place in the sixteenth century no pigsty was allowed in the city nor in the suburbs within sixty feet of a highway. Even then its removal could be enforced if it constituted a nuisance. In Birmingham, in the middle of the nineteenth century, there were 1,600 pigsties, and the report adds "cholera had centred around these places." (23) It would have seemed incredible to the rulers of Birmingham that in a neighbouring town nearly three hundred years earlier a man should have petitioned the authorities to order the removal of a swine-sty because the smell prevented people visiting his garden. (24) The authorities in the middle of the nineteenth century were unaware that these things could be regarded as a nuisance, (25) and the pig, banished from the town in the past, came back later to take the place of the scavenger.

The slaughter-house had also re-entered the town, for in Coventry "there is a slaughter-house with open cess-pool in the centre of the town." Ten years after the Commissioners' report there was an attempt to remedy this state of affairs, and it was made illegal to kill cattle in London, . . . in cellars. (26)

The Commission's reports show that pestilence had become a part of town life and not a "visitation." About one-sixth of the deaths in the town were from infectious diseases, about two hundred and fifty deaths occurring each year at Coventry from this cause. (27) Away from the filth of the town, people had a longer expectation of life, and the average age at death was forty, (28) as against twenty at Liverpool, (29) and under twenty-one at Nottingham. (30)

At the beginning of this chapter it was claimed that the authorities in the towns investigated had secured as great a measure of sanitation as was possible at the time. Now, after this brief survey and comparison of town life at a much later period, it may be added that if some period in town life must be labelled as a time of in-sanitation, then the nineteenth century should be chosen. Leland, the sixteenth-century traveller, went hundreds of miles and visited scores of towns before the condition of a single one called for adverse comment. (31) Entire ignorance of town *Records*, together with a hasty inference drawn from the prevalence of disease at the time, has enabled people to depict the period as being outstanding for its lack of sanitation. The town *Records* confute this view. A study of the cause and incidence of some of the sixteenth-century diseases will deter a person from hasty pronouncements on general questions of sanitation. Cause and effect are sometimes further apart than is usually thought. If this were not so, what might have been the fate of those thousands of people in the middle of the nineteenth century living in almost unprecedented conditions of filth?

It is unnecessary to stress some of the other points raised in the foregoing pages. In the twentieth century we have returned to many of the beliefs of the old town rulers. The *laisser-faire* theories of the eighteenth and nineteenth centuries have been discarded, and regulation and control are accepted methods. It is again considered to be a duty to care for the widow and orphan; the State attempts to provide for those without work, and education and medical aid are now provided free. Perhaps more important, we are beginning to realize that there may be "poor people" who are not paupers in the nineteenth-century sense. In short, in the twentieth century we are in spirit much nearer the sixteenth than the nineteenth century. With our much greater population, we may not have towns with the beauty and simplicity of Burford or Chipping Camden or other old sixteenth-century towns, but we recognize the ugliness of the industrial town, and have town-planning Acts and attempts to create garden cities.

A study of town *Records* will destroy many false conceptions of early conditions and give a truer insight into some of the social problems and achievements of the age. With their aid it is possible to get a clearer idea of the development of legislation, and especially of the social legislations of the Elizabethan age. Custom precedes law. Voluntary associations lead the way. The State through law comes in to establish, not to create. By means of town *Records* we see small communities experimenting, proving, and achieving, and later their successes become the basis of State legislation. In future the great social legislation of Elizabethan statesmen must be visualized against the background of steady endeavour and achievement of the provincial town authorities.

NOTES

1. Creighton, *Epidemics in Britain*, i. 331, 336.
2. *State of Large Towns and Populous Places*, Royal Commission, 1844–45.
3. *Ibid.*, Report ii. Part ii. App. 244.
4. *Ibid.*, Report ii. Part ii. App. 250.
5. *Ibid.*, 21.
6. *Ibid.*, Report i. App. 17.
7. *Ibid.*, Report ii. Part ii. App. 281.
8. *Ibid.*, Report ii. App. 53.
9. *Norwich Records*, ii. 339, 340, 341.
10. *State of Large Towns and Populous Places*, Royal Commission, Report i. App. 187.
11. *Ibid.*, Report ii. Part ii. App. 284.
12. *Ibid.*, Report ii. Part ii. App. 268, 282.
13. *Ibid.*, Report i. App. 15.
14. *Ibid.*, Report ii. Part ii. App. 284.
15. *Ibid.*, Report ii. 46.
16. *Ibid.*, Report ii. App. 51.
17. *Ibid.*, Report ii. Part ii. App. 268.
18. *Ibid.*, Report ii. App. 48.
19. *Ibid.*, Report i. App. 132.
20. *Ibid.*, Report ii. Part ii. App. 269.
21. *Ibid.*, 19.
22. *Ibid.*, Report ii. Part ii. App. 253.
23. *Ibid.*, Report ii. 41.
24. *Hist. MSS. Comm. Report* 13, App. Part iv. 314.
25. *State of Large Towns and Populous Places*, Royal Commission, Report ii. 41.
26. Simon, *Sanitary Conditions of the City of London*, 23.
27. *State of Large Towns and Populous Places*, Royal Commission, Report ii. Part ii. App. 262.
28. *Ibid.*, Report i. App. 139.
29. *Ibid.*, Report ii. Part ii. App. 55.
30. *Ibid.*, 255.
31. Leland, *Itinerary*, ii. 110.

PART OF A CENSUS. WHO WERE THE UNEMPLOYED?

Name	Age	Employment	Children	Relief	Condition
Robert Rowe . .	46	Glazier. No work	} 5 children. Daughter spins	No alms	Indifferent
Elizabeth Rowe .	—	Spins			
Agnes Nickoles, widow	40	Sews	—	No alms	Indifferent
John Hubbard . .	38	Butcher	} 2 children	No alms	Very poor
Margaret Hubbard .	30	Sells sauce			
Richard Gurgle . .	30	Glazier. No work	} 1 child. Their own house	No alms	Indifferent
Dorothy Gurgle . .	30	Spins			
Ann Bucke, widow .	46	Sauce-maker. Teaches children	2 children, 9 and 5 years. Work lace	No alms	Very poor
Margaret Turner widow	50	Spins. Helps others		No alms	V

Name	Age	Occupation / Condition	Children	Alms	Condition
Elizabeth Wretton, widow	40	Spins and helps others	—	No alms	Very poor
William Carter	22	Bad leg and without comfort. Can't work	—	No alms	Very poor
Thomas Pele	50	Cobbler	3 children. One, age 16, spins. Two, age 12 and 6, go to school	No alms	Very poor
Margaret Pele	50	—			
Richard Glaward	60	Labourer. Out of work	1 child	No alms	Indifferent
Margaret Glaward	60	Spins		No alms	Indifferent
Elizabeth Graye	36	Spins			
Edward Harman	38	Weaver. Lace	5 children. Eldest 2 spin	No alms	Very poor
Tamizan Harman	37	Spins			Indifferent
Margaret Hothe, widow	68	Spins and launders	1 child	—	—
Thomas Parson	36	Serving Man		No alms	Very poor
Ellen Parson	—	Spins			

PART OF A CENSUS. WHO WERE THE UNEMPLOYED?—*Continued*

Name	Age	Employment	Children	Relief	Condition
John Tarkes . . .	40	Cordiner. Out of work	} 2 children. Go to school	No alms	Indifferent
Alice Tarkes . . .	40	Sews			
Alizardee Tulbourne .	40	Tailor. Out of work	} 2 children, 1 lame. Both spin	2d.	Very poor
Agnes Tulbourne . .	40	Knits and helps others			
John Petingale . .	40	Labourer. Out of work	} 3 children, eldest age 9. Go to school	2d.	Very poor
Agnes Petingale . .	40	Knits and helps others			
Michaell Maste . .	26	Blacksmith. Out of work	} —	No alms	Very poor
Susan Maste . . .	26	Very sick			
Agnes Warner, widow	60	Sews	1 child	2d.	Very poor
John Bright . . .	30	Carpenter	} —	No alms	Very poor
Margaret Bright . .	30	Sews			
Christian Hunter,	38	Spins	2 children, 1 and 14 years.	No alms	Very poor

Name	Age	Occupation	Family	Alms	Condition
Elizabeth Brother, unmarried	40	Helps women	—	No alms	Very poor
Helen Hanworth, unmarried	40	Spins. Has bad leg	—	No alms	Very poor
Nicholas Fox	40	Linen Weaver. Out of work	} 3 children, eldest age 8. Eldest goes to school	2d.	Very poor
Agnes Fox	—	Spins			
Margaret Dunthorpe, widow	50	Spins	—	No alms	Very poor
John Byrde	30	Tailor. Out of work	} 1 child	No alms	Very poor
Margaret Byrde	20	Spins			
Barthelmew Matthews	60	—	} —	No alms	Very poor
Elizabeth Matthews	54	Spins			
Barthelmew Bell	40	Out of work	} 6 children. Eldest, age 10, spins	No alms	Lives in own house
Margaret Bell	36	Spins			

PART OF A CENSUS. WHO WERE THE UNEMPLOYED?—*Continued*

Name	Age	Employment	Children	Relief	Condition
John Bur	54	Very sick. Works not	7 children, age 20, 12, 10, 8, 6, 4, 2. Spin wool	No alms	Lives in own house. Indifferent
Alice Bur	40	Spins			
John Findley	82	No work	—	4d.	Very poor
Jone Findley	—	Sick, but spins and knits			
Elizabeth Tungut, widow	70	Spins	—	4d.	Very poor
Margaret Whitbread	80	Spins	—	4d.	Very poor
Robert Stutter	70	—		4d.	Very poor
Elizabeth Stutter	50	—			
William Dicer	60	Sawyer	2 children. Eldest age 9	No alms	
Alice Dicer	40	Spins			
John White	66	Labourer			
Cecelia White	—	Sick. Knits			Very poor

Edmund Todd Alice Todd	44 42	weaver Spins	} 3 children, age 13, 10, 6. Spin	2d.	Very poor
Roger Stevenson Jone Stevenson	52 52	Capper Spin and Cards	} 4 children. Eldest age 12	—	Indifferent
Katherine Downinge Christian Collard	60 40	Spins Knits	} —	No alms	Very poor
Cecelia Clue, widow	60	Knits	—	3d.	Very poor
Richard Newell Jone Newell	40 40	Tailor. Out of work Spins, Wash and Scours	} 3 children. Eldest age 7	No alms	Very poor
Richard Cacke Margaret Cacke	60 30	Labourer. Out of work Spins	} 2 children, age 8 and 6. Spin	2d.	Very poor
John Brice Ann Brice	40 28	Gardener. Out of work Spins	} 3 children. Eldest age 5	No alms	Poor
E. Barber Elizabeth Barber	36 33	Mouldmaker —	} 8 children, age 18, 17, 15, 13, 12, 9, 6, 4. Older spin	No relief	Indifferent

NOTES ON TOWN RECORDS

THE sources from which the foregoing particulars have been gathered can be divided into two groups. The first of these contain a number of town *Records* that have been translated or transcribed and printed at various times, some by interested individuals, some by interested societies, and others at the instance of the town authority concerned. The second group are publications issued by a Royal Commission which for over fifty years has been investigating the nature of the manuscripts preserved in the archives of various towns.

The latter section is important not only for what it actually presents, but also because of the immense amount of material to which it directs attention. The reports index documents which would enable the historian to reconstruct English social life over many centuries. It is not suggested here that the publications of this Commission are merely catalogues. Some of the reports have been exceedingly well done, but nevertheless from the point of view of the historian a great deal remains to be done in transcribing and translating many of the papers mentioned by the Commission. In their present form the publications of the Commission are a valuable source of reference, and have yielded much matter for this thesis. In that they record the existence of, and direct attention to, so much material, they are invaluable.

The first group consists of books varying greatly in value, most of which have been published within the last hundred years.

The question arises: "In what form should town *Records* be compiled?" Should the author use the *Records* to reflect the history of the town? or merely present the town *Records*? So far as the student of social history is concerned, the value of the work will depend upon the answer it gives to these questions.

In the books in this section, some authors have taken one view and some the other. The *Northampton Records* were published in 1898, and the author of the second volume stated that it would be distasteful merely to publish a transcript of the *Records* with little or no comment. So he grouped the main facts under suitable headings, and the whole, with the author's comments, forms an interesting sketch of bygone Northampton. It is, however, nothing more, for by doing the work in this way it has been rendered almost useless as a source-book for the historian.

Unfortunately many of the published town *Records* have been produced in the same form, and, like the *Northampton Records*, are interesting sketches of particular towns, but less valuable than they might have been. Some of the works to be placed in this group are Owen and Blakeway's *History of Shrewsbury* (1825), Turner's *Selections from the Records of the City of Oxford* (1880), Picton's *Selections from the Municipal Archives of Liverpool* (1885), and Morris's *Chester during the Plantagenet and Tudor Reigns* (1895). This last work so nearly fulfils the requirements of the student, that only the excellence of a few books that remain to be mentioned cause it to be placed in the second rank.

To be of value to the various people who approach social history from different angles, it is essential that there be in existence transcript copies of the actual *Records*, and if to transcribe page after page of the town *Records* is distasteful to an individual, then he is not the person for that kind of work. Fortunately some few people have realized that this should be done and have produced copies of town *Records* without expressing their own opinions or taking the responsibility of selecting what should be presented to the public. These books provide an almost inexhaustible store of material for the historian, and are of the greatest value. In social history the constitutional aspect has so dominated the outlook of the writers that we are far better informed on how things came to be than on how they served their purpose. But with the fuller transcripts it is possible to strike a balance, and while charters will enable students to understand the evolution and the constitution of a town Council, the publication of the "Minutes" of the Council meeting show what the Council and the people of the town were doing.

Of the older books that fulfil these requirements, first place must be given to Bacon's *Annals of Ipswiche* (1654), followed much later by Cooper's *Annals of Cambridge* (1843). The next work, Earwaker's *Court Leet Records of Manchester* (1884–90), gives the full transcript of the preserved *Records*. Two other works of equal value are *The Records of the Borough of Nottingham* (1880–90) and *The Records of the City of Norwich* (1908–10). Three other works, because of their excellence, deserve special notice, viz., *The Coventry Leet Book*, by Miss Mary Dormer Harris (1907–13), and *The Records of the Borough of Leicester*, edited by Mary Bateson and W. H. Stevenson (1899–1923), and Salter's *Oxford Council Acts*.

It is impossible to differentiate between these three works. In them the authors have adopted the method of presenting all the facts and leaving their selection and use to the student, and it is sufficient to add that these publications are excellent illustrations of how town *Records* should be reproduced.

A few general works by well-known authorities have been used to illustrate various points of view, or to furnish facts about which the town *Records* are silent. In addition, *Leland's Itinerary*, Harrison's *Description of England*, Clowes' *Book of Observations*, and Cogham's *Haven of Health*, are very important as giving contemporary evidence, while Creighton's *Epidemics in Britain* proved extremely useful for its medical opinion. The small book published by the Queen and Privy Council, and I believe not previously noticed, is valuable evidence of the anxiety of the authorities to collect and disseminate information about the plague, but it also shows that some of the provincial towns were far in advance of the central authorities.

AUTHORITIES QUOTED

BATH, The Municipal Records of. A. J. King and B. H. Watts. London. 1885.

BERWICK-ON-TWEED. History of the Town and Gild. John Scott. London. 1888.

BEVERLAC. George Poulson. London. 1829.

CAMBRIDGE, Annals of. Charles H. Cooper. Vols. i–ii. Cambridge. 1842–43.

CHESTER during the Plantagenet and Tudor Reigns. R. H. Morris. Chester. 1895.

COLCHESTER. Report on the Records of the Borough of Henry Harrod. Colchester. 1865.

COVENTRY, The Leet Book of. Mary Dormer Harris. Vols. ii–iii. 1908–9.

EXETER, History of. A. Jenkins. Exeter. 1805.

IPSWICHE, The Annals of. Nathaniel Bacon. Edited by W. H. Richardson. Ipswich. 1884.

LEICESTER, Records of the Borough of. Mary Bateson. Vols. ii–iii. Cambridge. 1901, 1905. W. H. Stevenson. Vol. iv. Cambridge. 1923.

LIVERPOOL. Selections from the Municipal Archives. From the thirteenth to the seventeenth century. Sir James A. Picton. Liverpool. 1883.

MANCHESTER, The Court Leet Records of. J. P. Earwaker. Vols. i–xii.

NEWCASTLE and GATESHEAD, A History of. From the fourteenth to the seventeenth century. Richard Welford. London and Newcastle.

NORTHAMPTON, Records of the Borough of. C. A. Markam. Vol. I. J. C. Cox. Vol. ii. Northampton. 1898.

NORWICH, Records of the City of. Rev. W. Hudson. Vol. i. John C. Tingey. Vol. ii. Norwich and London. 1906, 1910.

NOTTINGHAM, Records of the Borough of. W. H. Stevenson. Vols. iii–iv. Published for the Corporation, Nottingham and London. 1885, 1889.

OXFORD, Selections from the Records of the City of. W. H. Turner. 1880.

OXFORD. Council Acts. H. E. Salter. Oxford. 1928.

SHREWSBURY, A History of. H. Owen and J. B. Blakeway. London. 1825.

SOUTHAMPTON, Court Leet Records of. Professor Hearnshaw. Vol. i. Part i. Southampton. 1905.

TIVERTON, History of. William Harding. Vols. i–ii. Tiverton. 1845, 1847.

WINCHESTER. Transcripts from the Municipal Archives of, Charles Bailey. Winchester and London. 1858.

HISTORICAL MANUSCRIPTS COMMISSION'S REPORT ON TOWN RECORDS

BEVERLEY. London. 1900.

BRIDGNORTH. Report 10. App. Part iv. 1885.

CANTERBURY. Report 9. Part i. App. 1883.

CHESTER. Report 8. Part i. 1881.

COVENTRY. Report 15. App. Part x. 1899.

EXETER. London. 1916.

GLOUCESTER. Report 12. App. Part ix. 1891.

HEREFORD. Report 13. App. Part iv. 1892.

LINCOLN. Report 14. App. Part viii. 1895.

RYE. Report 13. App. Part iv. 1892.

SALISBURY. Report on Various Collections. Vol. iv. 1907.

SHREWSBURY. Report 15. App. Part x. 1899.

GENERAL AUTHORITIES QUOTED

Holy Trinity Church, Chester, Parish Registers of. Rev. L. M. Farral. Chester. 1914.

England, The Economic History of. Vol. i. Middle Ages. E. Lipson. London. 1915.

England, Harrison's Description of. Vol. i and ii. Furnival. London. 1877.

English Public Health, The Story of. Sir Malcolm Morris. London. 1919.

Epidemics in Britain, The History of. Charles Creighton. Cambridge. 1891.

Industry and Commerce, The Growth of English. "Mercantile, System." W. Cunningham. Cambridge. 1912.

Leland's Itinerary. Vols. i, ii, iii. Third Edition. Thomas Hearne. Oxford. 1768.

Norfolk, A History of. Vol. iii (Norwich). Frances Blomefield. London. 1806.

Wood's City of Oxford. A Clark. Oxford. 1889.

Plague, How to Recognize, Prevent, and Treat the. James Cantile. London. 1900.

Sanitary Conditions in London. John Simon. London. 1854.

State of Large Towns and Populous Places. Royal Commission, Reports i and ii. With Appendix. 1844–45.

Statutes of the Realm. 1810–22. Folio Edition.

OTHER WORKS

The Haven of Health. Thomas Cogham, M.A. Fourth Edition. London. 1636. (The Queen's College Library.)

A Profitable and Necessary Book of Observations. William Clowes. Third Edition. London. 1637. (The Queen's College Library.)

Stow's Chronicle. See "Three Fifteenth-Century Chronicles." Edited by Gardner. Camden Society. 1880.

ORDERS THOUGHT MEET BY HER MAJESTIE AND HER PRIVY COUNCIL

"to be executed throughout the counties of this Realm, in such towns and villages and other places, as are, or may be hereafter infected with the plague, for the stay of further increase of the same."

"Also an advice set down upon Her Majesties express Commandment By the best learned in Phisicke within this Realm, containing sundry good rules and easy medicines, without charge
to the meaner sort of people as well for the preservation of her
good subjects from the plague before infection, as for the curing
and ordering of them after they shall be infected."

Imprinted at London by the Deputies of
Christopher Barker
Printer to the Queen's Most Excellent Majestie
An. Don. 1593.

(Bodleian Library.)

INDEX

A Cultural History of the Modern Age

by EGON FRIEDELL

TRANSLATED BY CHARLES FRANCIS ATKINSON

Royal 8vo.   *In Three Volumes*   21s. *each*

Volume I: From the Black Death to the Thirty Years' War

Volume II: From the Thirty Years' War to the Congress of Vienna

Volume III: From the Congress of Vienna to 1914

"Hard, clear, brilliant, intelligent. . . . The studies of Wallenstein, Pascal, Descartes, Leibnitz, Frederick, Voltaire, Napoleon . . . and especially of Spinoza, are so brilliant as to convey the impression of profundity."—*Manchester Guardian*

A Short History of the World's Shipping Industry

by C. ERNEST FAYLE

Author of *Seaborne Trade*

Demy 8vo.   *With Eight Plates*   12s. 6d.

"A fascinating volume, dealing with the general history of shipping and British shipping in particular, 'from Coracle to Cunarder.' . . . Modern developments of shipping, its organization, the relative position of British shipping to that of the world as a whole, are all treated in masterly fashion."—*Morning Post*

The Religious Foundations of Internationalism

A Study in International Relations through the Ages

by NORMAN BENTWICH

Weizmann Professor of the International Law of Peace at the Hebrew University of Jerusalem

Demy 8vo.   10s. 6d.

"A very interesting and important book, made the more interesting and more important by the personality of its author."—*Church Times*

"A very stimulating book. . . . Mr. Bentwich writes well and temperately, and his book should be read."—*Spectator*

The Progress of International Government

by DAVID MITRANY, D.Sc., Ph.D.

Cr. 8vo.   5s.

This is a study of the gradual evolution of International Government. The author deals with his subject under the following headings: "International Government in Perspective," "Realities in State Equality," "The Communal Organization of World Affairs," "Authority in the World of States."

The Royal Empire Society
by AVALINE FOLSOM, M.A., Ph.D.

Demy 8vo. 10s. 6d.

The book treats of the part played by the Royal Empire Society in maintaining the integrity of the British Empire. It deals primarily with the first fourteen years of the Royal Colonial Institute when the Founders were labouring to dispel the generally prevalent ignorance about the colonies. Those early imperialists, whose pioneer efforts have been generally disregarded because of the greater fame of their successors, are accorded a tardy appreciation. There is also indicated the tremendous influence of the Society which has consistently chosen to work unobtrusively but steadily toward the goal of a mutual understanding among the various members of the British Empire. Different as is the Empire now from what was envisaged, it must be realized that its very existence is, to a large extent, attributable to the endeavours of the Founders of the Royal Colonial Institute.

Germany Under the Treaty
by W. H. DAWSON

Demy 8vo. *Maps* 10s. 6d.

"An important and a timely book. Mr. Dawson writes with recognized authority on German affairs, and those who look to him to explain the nature of the great wave of opinion which has carried Herr Hitler into power will not be disappointed."—*Times Literary Supplement*

"A book which all Englishmen would do well to read, especially just now . . . deserves to be carefully studied by all who would get a true insight into the dangerous situation existing in Middle Europe at the present time."—*Truth*

History of Germany
by HERMANN PINNOW

La. Cr. 8vo. TRANSLATED BY M. R. BRAILSFORD 12s. 6d.

"Does for Germany what Green's *Short History of the English People* did for England."—*Everyman*

"Particularly to be commended to the notice of the general reader, for it reveals Germany . . . with unusual clarity."—*New Statesman*

"An ably written survey of a thousand years of German history . . . provides a brilliant picture of the social and cultural no less than the political and economic life of the German peoples throughout a millennium."—*Times Literary Supplement*

Renascent India
by H. C. E. ZACHARIAS

Demy 8vo. *Frontispiece* 10s. 6d.

"*Renascent India* is a work of high value. . . . Dr. Zacharias has the honest broker's mind, which sees both sides in their merits and shortcomings, and believes in both and hopes to see both reconciled."—DR. EDWARD THOMPSON in *Spectator*

Whitehall at York

edited by J. BOWES MORRELL and A. G. WATSON
Foreword by Sir John A. R. Marriott

Demy 8vo. *Illustrated* 15s.

"The two volumes, this and its predecessor, form together a valuable contribution to the study of an amazingly intricate but vitally important phase of modern development."—*Sheffield Daily Telegraph*

"Should have a very wide appeal. It is a work very well done, deserving of imitation in other towns. . . . It is anything but a dry tome. It can be read with the relish of a novel."—*Northern Echo*

Bound uniform with this volume

How York Governs Itself

edited by J. BOWES MORRELL and A. G. WATSON

Demy 8vo. *Illustrated* 15s.

"This is an excellent book, portraying as in a mirror the actual working of the civic government of a city that has civic traditions that go back almost into pre-history."—*Times Literary Supplement*

The Old School Lists of Tonbridge School

by WALTER G. HART

Cr. 8vo. 6s.

Tonbridge School was founded in the year 1553 by Sir Andrew Judd, who by his will entrusted the school to the control of the Skinners' Company of London, of which he was a member and on six occasions Master. Among the records preserved by the Company at their hall there were discovered a few years ago a number of lists of the boys in the school at various times in the seventeenth, eighteenth, and early nineteenth centuries extending from 1654 to 1818. This book contains a short description of these lists with an account of a few of the more eminent men whose names appear in the lists, and of some of the leading families of Kent and Sussex who sent their sons to be educated at the school during the period covered by the lists.

Heart Burial

by CHARLES A. BRADFORD, F.S.A.

La. Cr. 8vo. 8s. 6d.

This is an essay and a collection of notes describing the ancient custom of the division of the human body at death and the separate disposal of its parts, as illustrated by cases within the London postal area. The notes on special cases of heart burial, which constitute the greater part of the book, range from the twelfth century to the twentieth, from Henry II to Thomas Hardy. The essay is based on patient research and contains much out-of-the-way matter of human and antiquarian interest. It is a book for the curious reader, the amateur of history and the antiquary.

GEORGE ALLEN & UNWIN LTD
LONDON: 40 MUSEUM STREET, W.C.1
CAPE TOWN: 73 ST. GEORGE'S STREET
SYDNEY, N.S.W.: WYNYARD SQUARE
TORONTO: 91 WELLINGTON STREET, WEST
WELLINGTON, N.Z.: 8 KINGS CRESCENT, LOWER HUTT